The
and
the Dove

Dr Katherine Lack graduated from Oxford in 1980. She is a freelance writer and lecturer in church history and has led a variety of tours to the Celtic sites of Britain. The field research for *The Eagle and the Dove* was done during an extended family holiday in Europe in spring 1998. Katherine Lack is married to a Church of England country parson, lives on the edge of the Welsh Marches and grows organic vegetables in her spare time.

Dedicated in memory of
Veronica Owen
1925–1999

The Eagle
and
the Dove

THE SPIRITUALITY OF THE CELTIC
SAINT COLUMBANUS

KATHERINE LACK

TRIANGLE

Published in Great Britain in 2000 by
Triangle
Society for Promoting Christian Knowledge
Holy Trinity Church
Marylebone Road
London NW1 4DU

British Library Cataloguing-in-Publication Data

A catalogue record for this book is available from the British Library

ISBN 0-281-05323-5

Typeset by Pioneer Associates, Perthshire
Printed in Great Britain by
Omnia Books Ltd, Bishopbriggs, Glasgow

Contents

List of Illustrations   vii
Acknowledgements   viii

Columbanus   xi

PART I THE EAGLE AND THE DOVE

1   Boyhood   3
2   Flee!   7
3   With Sinell at Cleenish   10
4   Bangor   16

PART II THE FLIGHT FROM IRELAND

5   The Celtic Sea   23
6   West Country Interlude   30
7   Around Brittany   35
8   Into France   43

PART III THE EAGLE IN FLIGHT

9   To the Frankish Court   51
10   In the Vosges   60
11   The Hermitage   64
12   Life at Luxeuil   68
13   Conflict with the Local Bishops   74
14   Conflict at Court   80
15   Exiled   85

PART IV UNDER THE SHADOW OF HIS WINGS

16	To the Court of King Lothar	97
17	Rowing up the Rhine	103
18	Detour to Lake Zurich	108
19	To Bregenz	112
20	Two Years in Bregenz	115
21	The Death of Brunhilda	119
22	Into Italy	123
23	At Milan	127

PART V AS A DOVE TO THE DOVECOTE

24	Bobbio	135
25	Peace at Last	141
	Appendix: Sermon I – Faith	142
	References and Further Reading	147

List of Illustrations

The Journeys of St Columbanus   2

The Frankish Kingdoms in the days of Columbanus   44

The early Merovingian Kings of France   46

The Southern Vosges   69

The influence of Columbanus: Monasteries under the
Columbanian Rule and sees occupied by his disciples   101

Acknowledgements

This book is the work of many hands. I have woven the final tale, but the threads were often supplied by others. To Canon Peter Kerr I owe a great debt, for awakening my interest in early Christian history. Without my husband Paul and above all my son Christopher, who is my sternest critic, I might never have completed the task. To the Revd Jackie Davies go my sincere thanks for patient and scholarly help with the nuances of the Latin texts on which our translations are based; I am grateful for her permission to use her work.

I acknowledge the generosity of the Governing Board of the School of Celtic Studies of the Dublin Institute for Advanced Studies for permission to base our translations of works attributed to Columbanus on their text of G. S. M. Walker's *Sancti Columbani Opera*. I would also like to acknowledge the kindness of Phillimore and Co. Ltd for allowing us to use their Latin edition of the works of Gildas, by Michael Winterbottom, for our translation of the section of his Letter No. 3.

I also acknowledge with gratitude permission to reproduce extracts from *The Chronicles of Fredegar*, by J. M. Wallace-Hadrill, published by Thomas Nelson Ltd. The extracts from Pliny's *Natural History* (translated by John F. Healy) and *The History of the Franks* (translated by Lewis Thorpe) are reproduced by permission of Penguin Books Ltd. The extracts from *Bede's Ecclesiastical History of the English People* (translated by Bertram Colgrave, 1969, and edited by Judith McClure and Roger Collins, 1999) are reproduced by permission of Oxford University Press. The extracts from *The Life of St Gall* (edited and translated by M. Joynt) and *The Life of St Samson of Dol* (edited and translated by T. Taylor) are reproduced with permission from SPCK.

Several people have read part or all of the manuscript, or assisted with their particular expertise. In particular I would like to thank Mary Calvert, Hugh Cullen, Margaret and the Rt Revd Philip Goodrich, Sally Jones, Philippe Kahn in Luxeuil, Maggie Kingston, Elizabeth Lack, Peter Lack, Helen Lanigan Wood at the Fermanagh County Museum, David Lovelock, Father James Murphy, Diana Ryan, Father Pat Sayles of the Columban Fathers in Co. Meath, Joan and John Taylor, Ian Wilson of the Bangor Heritage Centre in Co. Down, and the librarians at Tenbury Wells and the Bodleian, Oxford.

Columbanus

Before he was born, Columbanus' mother had a strange dream. She saw the sun rising up from her bosom and bathing the world in light, so that darkness was banished. Just how this story was remembered, years later and half a continent away, is a moot point, but the message is clear: Columbanus was a man of destiny, and those who knew him felt it.

St Columbanus was an extraordinary man even by the standards of his own times. Unlike his contemporaries – Columba of Iona, Ciaran of Clonmacnoise, Kevin of Glendalough – he cannot be tied down to one particular place. From Ireland to Italy he blazed a trail and changed lives. Consequently he is known by a variety of titles: Columbanus of Bangor, of Luxeuil or of Bobbio.

In the French Vosges and in Bregenz on Lake Constance stand matching statues of Columbanus, marking his passage across Europe, gaunt and unafraid. He was named for the dove, and he felt the dove's humility, but his contemporaries more often encountered him as an eagle, imperious, majestic and masterful.

In the years following Columbanus' death, an Italian monk called Jonas collected all he knew of his hero and recorded it for posterity in his *Life of Columbanus*. Jonas was not writing 'history' in the modern sense, of course, but using the life of Columbanus as a vehicle for glorifying God in contemporary terms, demonstrating the man's sanctity, and exalting the monastic foundations associated with him. Much remains obscure, but in the 'dark ages' Columbanus shines like a beacon from the west. From his actions and from his own surviving writings the man who emerges is very human, no cardboard-cut-out saint. His travels and his travails are equally vivid, as he battled with the elements, the courts of Europe and his own temperament.

Tracing Columbanus' footsteps today enables much to be filled in with informed guesswork: his journeys, his mode of life, something even of his motivation. But as in life, so in death; it is appropriate for the man to speak for himself:

O Lord God, tear down and root out whatever the enemy plants in me, that having destroyed all my iniquities, you may sow understanding and good work in my heart and mouth; so that I may serve you alone in deed and truth, and understand how to fulfil the commandments of Christ and seek your self only. Give me memory, give me love, give me purity, give me faith, give me every thing you know is beneficial for my soul.

O Lord, accomplish what is good in me and grant me what you know I need.[1]

Note

1 The Prayer of St Columbanus.

PART I

The Eagle and the Dove

The Journeys of St Columbanus

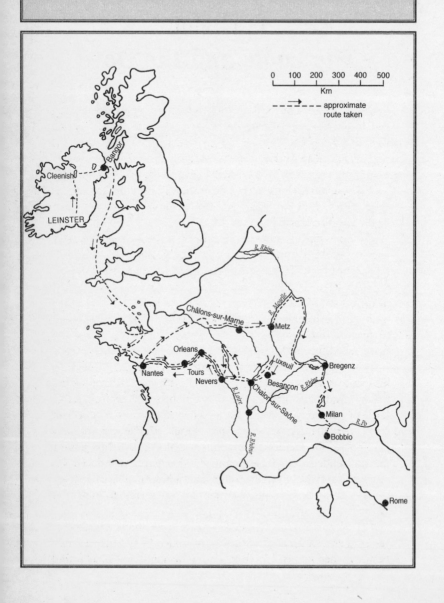

1
Boyhood

In about 542 AD, a boy was born to an Irish freewoman in the rich and lovely land of Leinster. She was a Christian, living among Christian neighbours and kinsfolk, in a tiny settlement deep in the countryside. Like all mothers, she was convinced that her son had a brilliant future, and his baptismal name was chosen with care. He was christened Columba, 'the dove', but his friends sometimes called him Colum Ban, the White Dove; later he was often known by the Latinized form Columbanus.

The dove was a symbol of much of the new Christian teaching, and it was a favourite name among the Christians of Ireland. It represented humility and purity, but also the huge and overpowering force latent in the Holy Spirit, the mysterious unseen element of the Christian God. The dove was an emblem both of hard-won peace and reconciliation, and of the soul regenerated through forgiveness. For many, it also symbolized the divine inspiration that created the great teachers and leaders of the churches.

Driven by her vision of her son's bright future, and inspired by his name, Columbanus' mother broke with the tradition of her relatives and peers, and refused to let him be sent away from home for his upbringing. Ignoring the raised eyebrows in the close-knit clan, where the decision of the senior male relative was normally paramount, she decided to raise him herself. One can only assume that any tendency towards spoiling that this may have induced was removed from the boy in the rough and tumble of village life: there is no evidence in his later years that he was unable to look after himself.

So Columbanus spent his earliest years under the watchful eye of his mother, in a rural settlement, surrounded by friends and relations who had known him from birth. The handful of small round huts of wattle and daub were clustered inside their embankments and protected with a thorn hedge or palisade. The narrow entrances could be sealed at night against wild animals or unfriendly neighbours. Within the enclosure, among the huts, was space to corral the livestock: the fine herd of cattle that was the family's pride, the occasional pigs, sheep and, of course, a roost for the chickens. Land was owned jointly by the kin-group, but inside their own enclosures, on the clay floors of the huts, families had a range of possessions pertaining to their domestic and agricultural lives: cooking pots and cauldrons of iron and bronze; a roasting spit standing by the hearth; mugs, bowls, spoons and knives; bedding and clothes of linen and wool; awls and axes; buckets for milking and carrying water.

As the boy grew up, he explored the cleared land surrounding the settlement, in the company of an assortment of dogs and other children. A considerable area of grassland provided pasturage for the herds and flocks, and hay for winter fodder. Fields were also ploughed, using draught oxen, and grew crops of flax, rye, wheat and oats. As soon as he was able, Columbanus began to help out in the fields, scaring away birds, gathering the sheaves at harvest, herding the livestock, and finding wild produce in its season: fruit, nuts and a whole variety of green plants. Soon, too, he was taught how to fish in the numerous rivers and lakes in the low-lying valleys, and how to hunt for the wild birds that formed an important part of their diet: geese, ducks, swans and many smaller species too. As he grew stronger, he was free to roam further away, into the fringes of the vast forests that covered most of the landscape, and to learn the lore of nature, discovering both the beauty and the hidden menaces of the wild.

It was a good place to grow up, well away from the coast with its danger of sea-raiders, and in a fertile and well-provisioned land. It was a good time, too. The advance of Christianity over Ireland was reducing the impact of the age-old horrors of cattle-rustling and slave-raids between kin groups, and Leinster was relatively peaceful under the overlordship of its high-king. In the spring, the meadows grew a fresh tapestry of glory, and in the autumn the haunting cries of the returning wildfowl marked the steady march of the seasons.

But the pre-Christian ways were not swept away overnight. St Patrick had been in his grave for only two generations, and despite the efforts of men like St Declan of Waterford, there were many pockets of paganism remaining, as well as many pagan assumptions. When the dreaded plague swept across Ireland in Columbanus' childhood, many wondered why the Christian god was powerless to save so many of his servants from being carried off in their prime. Columbanus' own father may have died of it; there is no mention of him in the boy's story.

As he grew up, Columbanus' mother took care that he attended to his book-learning as well as outdoor pursuits. If he was to have a bright future, he must be literate. So he went to study at a school, somewhere not too distant from home. Leinster was famous for its schools, and youths from many parts of Britain went there to learn. Columba of Iona, another 'dove', may have come down from Donegal in the north to 'study divine wisdom' at the schools of Finnian and Gemman at much the same time as Columbanus was going to school.[1] First, the new pupil had to master the basics of literacy. Wax tablets and hours of patient study enabled him to learn the Latin alphabet, and then he learnt to read and write, using the Psalter as his primer. Before long, he had committed the whole book to memory, and was able to study the Gospel of John and other parts of the Bible.

In St John, the Eagle of the evangelists, he became aware of a new vision. The early Irish churches were entranced by the imagery and power of that Gospel. Together with the Psalter, it was the book most often copied and most frequently carried on journeys. It was given as a gift and studied as words of gold. The beauty of the language and the soaring of its thought reminded Columbanus of the golden eagles watching high above the hills of Leinster, of the fish eagles swooping and soaring on confident outspread wings, the ospreys plunging down to the waters of the lakes, sharp-eyed, exact and miraculous. The dove and the eagle met in his studies, and began to take wing.

Grammar, rhetoric, geometry and the Holy Scriptures; this was the curriculum considered necessary to equip a well-to-do young Irishman for his future. Perhaps his mother expected that he would in due course obtain a position as a wise man among his aristocratic relations, thanks to his literacy in the new learning. In due course, he might donate land for the foundation of a monastery, or be ordained and selected as a bishop to preside over the lands ruled by his kinsman, in the old way. What neither Columbanus nor his mother expected was that anything dramatic would interfere with his studies.

Note

1 Adomnan, *The Life of St Columba*, II.1 and II.25 (*c.* 690 AD) (Sharpe, 1995).

2

Flee!

as his fine figure, his splendid colour, and his noble manliness made him beloved by all, the old enemy began finally to turn his deadly weapons upon him.[1]

Columbanus left adolescence behind him and woke up to discover that he was a good-looking young man. Moreover, the local girls had made the same discovery. Pursuer soon became pursued. If it was his destiny to become a priest, marriage was no bar. But his teachers were encouraging him to think about entering one of the new monastic communities, as a celibate monk. The light-hearted fun of the chase gave way to real uncertainty about where his future lay.

As Columbanus contemplated the future, and tried to imagine life devoid of all the charms and challenges of secular living, he happened upon a small hermitage where an old woman lived alone, praying and meditating on her Scriptures. In appearance, it was just like his mother's hut at home, and the soul that inhabited it was even more clear of purpose, and outspoken in her vision. Like so many other Irish of her generation, the woman had been seized by a desire to renounce her past life and make a fresh start as a symbol of her dedication to the new faith. As Columbanus talked with her, she told him that her desire had been to leave Ireland and travel overseas to fulfil her vow to forsake her home and kinsfolk for Christ. But, to her shame, she had not dared to do so, and had opted instead for the lesser exile of living in the wilderness, far away from home in a land of strangers.

'But you,' the anchoress told Columbanus, 'glowing with the fire of youth, stay quietly on your native soil; out of weakness you lend your ear even against your own will, to the voice of the flesh, and think you can associate with the female sex without

7

sin . . . Away, O youth! away! flee from corruption.'² Her words
struck home. He was well aware that he was attracted to the young
women he had met while studying, and knew how close he was
to an irrevocable step. He was also strongly attracted by the confidence the old woman showed in her faith, her practical reliance on
the actual truth of the words she read in the Bible. He recognized
and admired her strength of character, for her way of life was no
idyll: the forests of Leinster were not a safe place for a woman,
especially one living alone and far from the protection of relatives.
He knew that many others were opting for this kind of life, too.
Up in the Wicklow mountains to the north-east, a high-born man
named Kevin had withdrawn into a narrow wooded valley and
built himself a hermitage just as this woman had done. For Kevin,
the renunciation had been of the status and security to which he
had been born. His reputation for piety and wisdom was already
spreading, and he was finding it impossible to remain alone. Several
young men had already attached themselves to him, and the valley
began to take on the air of an informal religious community. But
whether alone or in a group, Columbanus could see that the religious
life was not a soft option. Rather, it began to look like a far greater
challenge than the sort of future he had been vaguely contemplating
up until then.

Taking leave of the anchoress gratefully, Columbanus returned
to his school, his mind made up. Having mastered the basics of
what could be taught him there, he was moving on. So he bade his
startled companions farewell, said he would not be coming back,
and went home.

Explaining to his mother was not so readily done. Whatever
golden future she had imagined for her boy, she had not thought
that it might involve him leaving Leinster. But this he was now
determined to do. He had decided to leave home, and study at
one of the new monasteries further north. Several of them, he
had heard, already had reputations as hard schools of discipline
as well as distinguished academic centres. At such a place he could
continue the studies which he loved, learn more music in which
he took great delight, and strive to tame his youthful inclinations
into obedience.

His mother did not understand. Why could he not continue his studies nearer to home? Why this sudden urge to leave Leinster? She had no husband; who would take care of her in her old age if he was far away?

But Columbanus had made up his mind. With the clarity and callousness of youth, he asked her not to stand in his way. Not to stand in God's way. He needed the broader experiences of the bigger monasteries of the midlands and the north. There were many to choose from, reflecting the different approaches of their founders: Kildare, Durrow, Clonard and Clonmacnoise in the midlands; or the northern foundations at Armagh, Moville, Derry, Bangor, Devenish and many more. Some already had a long and distinguished history, others, like Durrow and Bangor, were only newly founded and full of the enthusiasm and fire of a fresh beginning.

His mother went down on her knees and wept at the thought of him leaving her. Columbanus knew that she was well provided with relatives who could care for her, otherwise he would not have considered entering a monastery. He asked her to let him leave. He begged her not to upset herself. Mindful of Jesus' demand that his followers must be willing to give up their parents and all they love best, he steeled himself and prepared to go. She flung herself across the doorway, holding the door. Then, Columbanus stepped over her recumbent form, and walked away from the home he had known and loved all his life, warning his mother not to expect to see him again.

Notes
1 Jonas, 7 (Munro, 1895).
2 Jonas, 8 (Munro, 1895).

3

With Sinell at Cleenish

Lough Erne is in County Fermanagh; but in winter, Fermanagh is in Lough Erne.

(Local saying)

The 560s were a decade of power in the Irish churches. All over the midlands, young men and women were flocking to the new monastic schools, or setting out to found new communities of their own. As the young Columbanus walked north, he soon heard tales of the heroism of the founders and pioneers, and of the challenges of the life he had vowed to enter. At the monasteries associated with Finnian of Clonard, he would have heard of a remarkable man named Sinell, who combined scholarship with quite extraordinary gifts as a teacher. Like a dozen other men, Sinell had recently left the midlands, and had founded a small monastic school on an island in Lough Erne. To Lough Erne, then, Columbanus decided he would go, to ask to become one of Sinell's pupils.

With guides to show him the way over the often treacherous ground, Columbanus made his way north. The fertile, well-drained pastures of Leinster and the dry land around Kildare soon gave way to damper regions, where a path had to be picked with care. In places, the most frequented routes were marked by wooden trackways, but elsewhere the paths were small and obscure. Forest and grassland gradually gave way to marshy fens and increasingly frequent lakes and ponds. To the experienced traveller, it was an easy matter to identify the safe routes along the thin ridges of gravelly soil, but to the unwary some places were a death trap, with pockets of oozing bog, adorned with deceptively beautiful cotton grass, waiting to suck the traveller in to his death. For the sensitive Columbanus, the whole journey was a parable of life. His mother's sobs still rang in his ears, and haunted him for weeks. Had he done right to abandon her? Was this quest of his the will of God, or a selfish deceit like the flowers of the bogs? Could the communities of the north help him find a path through life?

Further north still, hummocky hills began to rise above the marshy ground, and then the lowest lying areas began to be filled with larger areas of open water, alive with ducks of all kinds, and stately swans, enamel-blue kingfishers, crested divers and long-legged birds of many types, fishing or wading round the margins. From here on, the trees made land travel less easy and Columbanus took to the water, hitching lifts in dug-outs or in the strange flat bottom punts that the local people used to carry their livestock and other goods from one island of dry land to the next. Eventually, the River Erne formed itself lazily from an accumulation of ponds and streams and began its leisurely, meandering course towards the sea, rush-fringed and dotted with islands, many crowned by a settlement, secular or religious. Gradually the river widened and became a lough, scattered with yet more islands, and half-way up the long lough, where it narrows so that it is almost split in two, he came at length to Cleenish Island, a green mound rising whale-backed close by a deep channel. There, overlooking the waterway, was the monastic school of Sinell.

Here the young Columbanus spent his formative years. His life became forever moulded by the monastic discipline, summoned every three hours from work or sleep to prayers in the tiny church. His days revolved around the prayer bell, his weeks around the regular sequence of chanted psalms and canticles, his years around the great festivals of the church.

But Sinell son of Mianiach was more than just a good abbot. He was a shrewd judge of character and a relentless teacher. He took an interest in Columbanus, and pushed him to extend his studies, developing his natural aptitude for music and his love of the Scriptures. By testing the young man's determination, he drew out his native confidence and instilled in him a self-confidence and faith that could weather storms. For Columbanus, his relationship with God became close and real, and he came to believe passion-ately in the teaching of the Christian church. All around him, he could see proof of its truth. The psalms resonated so finely with the lot of man; the sacred story of redemption was mirrored perfectly in the recent history of his own Ireland. From the chaos of pagan society, where men worshipped the gods whom they did not know, Christianity was bringing forth a new society of hope.

Under Sinell's guidance, Columbanus wrote a commentary on the Book of Psalms, much admired at the time and probably preserved into the Middle Ages, but now sadly lost.[1] He also indulged his love of music by composing sacred songs to intersperse with the psalms and prayers of the community services. The Irish poem known as the 'Hymnum Apostolorum' (or the 'Precamur Patrem' from its opening phrase in Latin) has recently been attributed to him: it survives in a single copy, in the *Antiphonary of Bangor*, and is a work of beautifully crafted metre and rhyme probably intended for use at the long vigil on Easter Eve.[2] It reverberates with complex scriptural allusions and speaks of the composer's immense but humble confidence in the divine love:

> We pray to the Father, High King of great merit,
> And Jesus Christ and the Holy Spirit. Alleluia.

> We worship God, pure being is He,
> The three in one and one in three.
> The Light of all the orbs that shine,
> The very light at fount of time.

> This day the Daylight shone from heav'n,
> The Firstborn to the earth was given.
> The word made flesh since time began,
> Eternal light from God to man.

> He came into our lower world
> And powers of darkness back were hurled.
> And he subdued the ancient foe,
> And death's cruel fetters he let go.

> Where all before was darkest night,
> Now shone the first-born rays of light.
> Once mortal hearts in blindness lay,
> But now the True Light shows the Way.

As on this day at the Red Sea,
Israel from Egypt went out free;
So may we leave life's havens too,
And in the desert strive to go.

With foes destroyed, all Israel vied
To praise the Lord their fiery guide.
Though worthless, praising God we must
Cast down our foe into the dust.

And in this Fount of Light adored,
Behold God's liberating Word.
Praise God for light from heaven above,
Praise for faith's ardent flame of love.

Myst'ries too deep for human tongues,
The Saviour in His mercy comes.
Now all displayed here, plain to see,
As prophets said that it would be.

Housed here on earth, born man to die,
Yet still in heaven in Trinity.
Druids adore the crying boy,
His star shines brightly in the sky.

In dirty cow-byre He was bound,
Who cradles all things in His hand.
To his disciples gave a sign,
Turned water into heavenly wine.

And as foretold by prophet's art,
The lame leapt nimbly like a hart.
And tongues were loosed and speech was heard
At the commanding of the Lord.

The blind, the deaf and lepers saved,
He raised up dead men from the grave.
He lifted up five loaves and then
With each loaf fed a thousand men.

But all this kindness from our Lord
Roused envy in the hostile horde.

Who looked askance and hated Him,
Who still to heaven prayed for them.

And soon the councillors decide
Great Council's Messenger must die.
Swords, robber-like, a prisoner find,
Yet He the Thief in hell will bind.

Now handed over, judged by men,
The King Eternal they condemn.
Sky crashed as He was crucified;
The sun was blackened as He died.

Rocks burst and torn the temple veil,
Dead men from tombs came fit and hale.
Six thousand years Adam was bound,
His torments end and he is sound.

From apple's death and life's fierce pain,
The first man rises free again.
This paradise, once lost to man,
By God's great mercy new began.

With Christ our Head now raised on high,
The Church is blessed in Trinity.
At His command, the heavenly door
Is opened wide for evermore.

The sheep are on their own Lamb's arm,
The straying one is kept from harm.
We look for him to come again,
The Judge in equity for men.

So awesome is your gift this day,
How can we hope our debt to pay?
Can mortal souls, in human word,
Declare the marvels of the Lord?

This blessing we beg you to pour out upon us;
Eternal God, have mercy upon us. Alleluia.[3]

Cleenish was not a quiet retreat. Lough Erne was no backwater, but one of the main north-south highways of Ireland. The area was a hive of activity. On dozens of nearby islands and promontories, small communities were growing up, each founded on the same basic impulse, but each reflecting the character of their founder. Sinell of Cleenish, Molaise of Devenish, Ninnidh of Inishmacsaint, Fainche of Rossory, Mochaimoc of Inishkeen, Tighernach of Derryvullan and Galloon, Senach of Derrybrusk, Machomma of Drummully, Naile of Kinawley, and many more. Each was conveniently situated near the waterways of Lough Erne, or one of the rivers which fed it, and their independence was tempered by the traffic that flowed past them, and the stream of travellers that came to their doors.

Thus it was that Columbanus came to hear about another community, far away on the east coast. It had been set up ten years previously, by a man named Comgall, who had himself spent time on one of the islands in Lough Erne. Back in his native north-east, Comgall had founded a great monastery – the Beannchor Mor, modern Bangor, on the Belfast sea lough.

The challenge of a monastery already renowned for combining scholarship with a strong ascetic tradition appealed to Columbanus' idealism. After several years in Sinell's school, he began to long to leave the soft green world of Fermanagh and join Comgall's followers. So, a vigorous young man in his twenties, to Bangor he determined to go.

Notes

1 Volume I was recorded in the ninth-century catalogue of the St Gallen library, Switzerland; volume II was recorded in the tenth-century catalogue of the Bobbio library, northern Italy. It is possible that all remaining copies were lost when the Bobbio library was divided between Milan and Rome under Pope Paul V (1605–1621).

2 See Lapidge (1997). For the Latin text, see Adamson, *Bangor, Light of the World*.

3 Hymnum Apostolorum (Precamur Patrem) from the *Antiphonary of Bangor* c. 690 AD.

4

Bangor

Good Rule of Bangor, holy, true and best;
Divine and constant, wonderful and blessed.
O House of Bangor, faith's foundations sure,
Adorned in hope and love for evermore.
A ship, though wave-tossed, never yet in fear;
A bride made ready, for her Lord is near.[1]

Comgall was one of the great men of Columbanus' time. Born into a noble family in south Antrim in about 515 AD, he elected to travel south to train for the religious life under the austere Fintan at Clonenagh. There, extreme asceticism was the rule. Fintan himself was reputed to live exclusively on barley bread and water, and he required a rigorous vegetarian discipline of his monks: not even milk was permitted. The regime at Clonenagh had nearly proved too much for the young Comgall. He became depressed and listless, and doubted his ability to live up to the standards required. But eventually, guided by Fintan, he travelled up to Lough Erne with a small group of companions, to test his vocation. So harsh was the life they adopted there that seven of the monks are said to have died of cold and hunger.

Returning to the north-east, Comgall was ordained priest and spent some time travelling round, perhaps as an itinerant preacher. In his early forties, he conceived an ambition to go abroad, as a 'wanderer for Christ', but was persuaded to remain in Ireland. Instead of pilgrimage overseas, he gathered a small group of men together and founded Bangor,

> in the Ards of Ulster, beside the eastern sea. And a great host of monks came there to Saint Comgall, so that they could not all

be in one place. And so he founded several cells and many monasteries, not only in Ulster, but through all the provinces of Ireland. And in the scattered cells and monasteries three thousand monks were under the care of the holy father Comgall.[2]

One of these young hopefuls seeking admission to Bangor was Columbanus. Leaving behind the Fermanagh wetlands, his best route lay north-east up the Fury valley, with the ridge of Slieve Beagh on his right. Beyond Armagh, with its monastery and proud associations with St Patrick, he would have skirted round the north Armagh boglands. Four days' travel brought him to the finger of higher land that ran down towards the great sea lough. As he came to its end, he saw the sea for the first time: an impressive sight, whether storm-tossed or sparkling in the sunshine. The broad lough, so different from the reed-fringed inland sea of Fermanagh, was ringed with high hills to the north, and small boats crept about on its surface near the bay below him.

> Others there are who go to sea in ships;
> plying their trade on the wide ocean.
> These have seen what the LORD has done,
> his marvellous actions in the deep.
> They rejoiced because it was calm,
> and he guided them to the harbour they were making for.
>
> (Psalm 107.23–24, 30)

In a sheltered valley, a kilometre from the little harbour, stood Comgall's Bangor. All that remains today is a trace of the earthworks of the enclosing ditch, but when Columbanus went there that ditch enclosed numerous wattle huts for the monks, several small wooden chapels, and the communal buildings: workshops, school-room, bakery and mill. The millstream is mostly now channelled underground, but its course is marked by Southwell Road, running down to the harbour.

Applying for admission, Columbanus was first housed in the guest hall, while his sincerity was tested. Later, aided perhaps by the portfolio of songs and commentaries he had brought with him from Cleenish, he was permitted to join in with the worship

of the community, and after a probationary period of several
months he was admitted. As a mark of his full acceptance he was
tonsured in the Celtic fashion 'from ear to ear' across the front of
his head. From then on, he was bound in obedience to his seniors
and ultimately to Comgall himself. Whatever he was commanded
to do, he was to do it immediately, humbly and without question.
Whatever his task, he was to do it with patience as if doing it for
God alone. Whenever he was rebuked, whether guilty or not, he
was to kneel and ask forgiveness.

The days were divided between manual labour in the fields and
gardens and book work indoors. But through them all, just as at
Cleenish, were threaded the hours of prayer. Eight services a day,
every day, throughout the year. Columbanus delighted in the
hard outdoor work, he loved the regular round of worship, with the
brothers' voices blending with the accompanying music, and above
all he revelled in the challenge of the work of the schoolroom
and scriptorium. Even the frugal diet was no real hardship to him,
inured as he was already to simple and sparse fare. At Bangor,
they ate one meal a day, in the late afternoon, and while Comgall
had relaxed from the severity of Fintan enough to allow a variety
of vegetables, and milk for the elderly or sick, no animal products
were on the regular menu.

Columbanus did not remain an inconspicuous newcomer for
long. Even in a monastery the size of Bangor, where the number
of brothers probably ran into hundreds, his zeal and particularly
his academic gifts were noticed. He was probably ordained priest
when he was thirty, and was soon put into a position of some
responsibility in the monastic school. By the time he was in his
early thirties, the fame of the Bangor school was beginning to be
associated with his name as well as with Comgall's. One couple
reputedly heard of him from far away south Leinster: '. . . the parents of the blessed Gall, persons devout in the sight of God and
honourable in the sight of men. They, offering their son in the
flower of early youth as a sacrifice to the Lord, entrusted him to
the teaching of Columbanus, that he might be trained in the religious life.'[3] Columbanus took the young Gall under his wing, and
taught him grammar, poetry, scriptural studies and theology, and

prepared him for the priesthood. It would be nice to think, despite the lack of evidence, that through Gall's family some news of Columbanus filtered back to his mother, in distant Leinster.

By now it was about 585 AD, and Columbanus had turned forty and risen to a position of great trust in Comgall's 'family'. He occupied a post akin to that of a prior, perhaps with oversight of the main Bangor community as well as his teaching duties. Columbanus the dove was peaceful, content within the framework of the Bangor Rule he had come to love so well. To Comgall's monks, their monasteries were more than just human institutions; they were a mirror held up to heaven, as they so vividly expressed in their 'Versicles of Bangor': their Rule was a safe ship in life's storms, a royal house and a Bride prepared for God, the source of the Cup of Salvation, the archetype of the New Jerusalem, the Ark of the Covenant made new, the sheepfold of Christ, obedient and submissive as Mary and yet the Queen of Heaven, the gateway to everlasting life.[4]

Within this community, Columbanus had a rigorous life, satisfying work and the privilege of seeing pupils like Gall mature into the next generation of church leaders. Yet, as his hair began to recede from his tonsure, he began to feel unsettled. Like Comgall and Columba before him, as he entered his forties so he longed to leave Ireland and cut loose from the earthly ties that bound him. The eagle felt pinioned, and needed to fly.

Columbanus went to Abbot Comgall and asked his permission to leave Bangor, in order, as he said, to follow God's call to Abraham to 'leave thy country and thy kindred and thy father's house and go to a land that I will show thee'. But Comgall refused. He was hoping that Columbanus would be in Bangor to be his comfort in his old age, and maybe to succeed him as abbot. He must also have been reluctant to lose such a bright jewel in Bangor's crown. Perhaps, too, he remembered how he himself had begged to be allowed to leave Ireland and be a wanderer for Christ, and how his elders had dissuaded him.

Columbanus was not easily put off. As the months went by, his resolution hardened. Bangor had been a vital phase in his life. It had largely made him what he was. But though trained in the dove's humility, his spirit needed to soar. He went to Comgall again and repeated his request, still more earnestly. This time, after careful thought, Comgall gave him his blessing, and encouraged Columbanus to take a band of brothers from Bangor with him on his travels, for 'although sorrowful, he considered the good of others before his own good.'[5]

The creed used at Bangor

I believe in God the Almighty and Invisible Father, Creator of all that is, both visible and invisible.

And I believe in Jesus Christ, His only Son our Lord, Almighty God, who was conceived by the Holy Spirit, born of the Virgin Mary, suffered under Pontius Pilatus, who was crucified and buried and descended into hell. On the third day he rose from the dead, ascended into heaven, and sat down at the right hand of God the Father Almighty, from whence he will come to judge the living and the dead.

And I believe in the Holy Spirit, Almighty God, having one substance with the Father and the Son.

And in the holiness of the universal church, the remission of sins, the communion of the saints, and the resurrection of the body.

I believe in life after death, and life everlasting in the glory of Christ.

All this I believe in the name of God. Amen.[6]

Notes

1 Opening lines of the 'Versicles of Bangor', from the *Antiphonary of Bangor*, c. 690 AD.
2 *The Life of St Comgall*, 13 (Latin text in Plummer, 1910).
3 *The Life of St Gall* by Walahfrid Strabo, I (ninth century) (Joynt, 1927).
4 Paraphrased from the 'Versicles of Bangor', in the *Antiphonary of Bangor*.
5 Jonas, 9 (Munro, 1895).
6 From the *Antiphonary of Bangor*.

PART II

The Flight from Ireland

5

The Celtic Sea

So they embarked, and began the dangerous journey across the channel and sailed quickly with a smooth sea and favourable wind to the coast of the Britons.[1]

So Columbanus set off; but not exactly into the unknown. The sixth-century seas were a regular highway between Ireland and her neighbours, largely untroubled by the marauding Saxon pirates who disrupted the North Sea trade. Many goods, pottery, fine luxury wares and even such vital necessities as the oil and wine for the sacraments of the church were imported from Gaul and the Mediterranean. In the other direction flowed hunting dogs, skins, slaves and Irish gold. There were also numerous contacts between the religious communities of the Celtic world. Columbanus' near contemporary Samson, for instance, was taught in Glamorgan, moved to Pembrokeshire and then the Wye valley, visited Ireland and spent some time in Cornwall and the Channel Islands before the last phase of his life in Brittany and Normandy. So it is safe to assume that the little group of companions knew by hearsay about the voyage ahead, and that several of them had made at least part of it before.

Jonas is clear about the number of people in the party: 12 besides Columbanus himself. This may be a literary convention; all the best saints copied their Master by setting out with 12 disciples. But it is also quite probably true. It was both a conscious imitation of Jesus and an excellent size for a group that would need to work together in various ways. Jonas mentions several of the group by name (one or two were still alive when he was collecting material for his book, and he met them himself); tradition and other sources add the names of the others. There were Gall and his older brother Deicola, from south-east Ireland; Comininus, Eunocus and Equanacus, three 'Scots', probably from Ulster or modern Argyll; Gurganus, a Briton, perhaps from Wales; another Columbanus, sometimes known as 'the younger'; Lua and Potentius; Aedh, who was a bishop, and two Saxons called Leobard and Caldwald, drawn to Christianity by some unknown route from their pagan kinsfolk before Augustine had even landed in Kent.

How did they travel? The conventional image of a crew of impractical but trusting Irish saints bobbing about in a little tub of a coracle will have to be discarded. These boats, noted by Pliny as 'coracles constructed of osier covered with sewn hides'[2] are ideal for use on inland waters. They float safely in a few inches of water, are stable with two or three people on board, yet can be made by skilled hands in two days, and carried about with ease. But for long sea crossings they are out of the question. There is a distinction between a child-like faith in the Almighty's protection and putting him to the test with acts of deliberate foolhardiness; a dozen monks in a coracle on the Atlantic comes into this category if anything does.

A more likely vessel for the voyage was a curragh, a sort of big brother of the coracle. Built with a central wooden rib fore and aft, and covered with up to 50 tough, oak-tanned ox hides, these small ships were designed for journeys on the open sea. The most reliable means of propulsion may have been rowing, sitting on cross thwarts, but there were also one or two square-rigged masts, a main and a fore-sail. Tim Severin, in his reconstruction of St Brendan's legendary voyages in the North Atlantic, concluded that for long journeys, the sails would be used wherever possible. Severin's vessel was over 11 metres long and nearly two and a half metres in the beam, with a sail area of about 19 square metres.[3] She could be handled under sail with a following wind by a crew of four, but effective rowing needed eight men. A smaller curragh[4] was built in 1997 and rowed to Iona for the 1400th anniversary of St Columba's death; she was 6.8 metres long, and took a crew of seven.

Into their ship, drawn up on the sand in the little bay at Bangor, Columbanus and his companions loaded their luggage for the voyage. By modern standards they took absurdly little for themselves;

a leather book satchel for their psalters and gospels, a flask for drinking water and maybe a knife or bowl. They wore a simple outer garment of undyed wool or linen, and their apron-like scapulas, and leather shoes. Excavations on Iona found the remains of shoes from just this period; strong, practical working shoes with attractive patterns stamped on them. For the party as a whole, several other things were needed; the *Voyage of Brendan* lists 'spare skins [for repairing the boat], forty days' supplies, fat for water-proofing the skins, tools and utensils.'[5] The food for a crossing to Gaul need only be simple: cheese, bread and maybe some vegetables or nuts. They also took a small cauldron for communal cooking and perhaps a travelling altar and communion set for their first weeks on foreign soil. For maintaining the boat they would take several tanned and trimmed oxhides, leather thongs and stitching equipment, and whale or sheep grease for sealing the seams. Possibly they also took the precaution of carrying a second supply of grease or oil, in case of bad weather. The Irish navigators knew that a trail of grease behind a curragh as she is blown before a storm helps to smooth the waves. The seventh-century bishop Aidan used this knowledge to help a boatload of Saxons, when 'waves swept over the ship from all sides; the vessel began to fill and they all realised that death was imminent and that their last hour had come, when the priest, remembering the bishop's words, took out the flask and poured some of the oil into the sea. At once, as Aidan had predicted, the sea calmed down.'[6]

At last Columbanus and his party were ready to leave. With Abbot Comgall's blessing ringing in their ears, and the singing of their brothers' farewell calling to them across the bay, they carefully poled their vessel out into deep water, and bent to the slender oars until it was safe to let the steady northerly wind fill their sails. Before they were settled, they had drawn so far away from the shore that Bangor was a distant patchwork on the darker green land around, and the long wide mouth of the lough was ushering them out into the sea.

The voyage down the Irish Sea reads like a history of the Christian communities around its shores. At first, they were sheltered by the familiar shapes of the hills to the north, but as they drew east they passed into the deeper waters of the North Channel, where the elements can combine to make conditions that even modern vessels avoid. But on this occasion, the weather was favourable, with a moderate following wind and tide, and they went steadily on their way. Standing over towards the British shore, in the early morning light they could soon make out the small cleft in the low cliffs, the harbour of Port Patrick, where so many Irish monks had landed on their way to Kirkmadrine and the green lands around Whithorn. Whithorn, the great international school where so many, men and women alike, went to study. So important was it that the name of Ninian, its founder, who had travelled as far as Rome 200 years before, and had himself sat at the feet of Martin of Tours, was still held in awe by the Irish churches.

The majestic Mull of Galloway faded into the distance, and all through the middle of the day they sailed on, past the Isle of Man, singing the afternoon office as the cliffs slipped slowly by. Late afternoon saw the southern tip of the island behind them, and then for a while they were alone on the open sea. Far out of sight to their right, they knew, was Ireland, but they did not expect ever to see her again. This pilgrimage was to be a one-way voyage in the hands of God, the pattern of their lives.

As night fell, they could see ahead of them the holy island of St Cybi, who had founded his settlement in the ruins of an old Roman fort. By then it was already a sizeable monastery, one of several on Anglesey; it attracted recruits from a wide area, in a land that had exchanged the relative security of Pax Romana for the uncertainties of tribal rule and foreign incursions. Well might the little band of travellers sing the familiar words of their evening office with extra fervour:

> Now in peace I shall lie down and sleep;
> for it is you alone, LORD, who let me live in safety.
>
> (Psalm 4.8)

All through the short summer night they continued southward, blown on at a steady pace by the kind wind. There is nothing inherently improbable in a moderate sea and a north-westerly force five, but to have it just when you want it, when the tides are right and the boat is ready, is something of a miracle: a miracle of timing. No doubt they had a change of helmsman at the long steering oar, and used the opportunity to sing the night office, while the boat ploughed on over the waves, under the stars and moon.

> For the LORD is a great God,
> a great King above all gods.
> The depths of the earth are in his hands,
> and the peaks of the mountains belong to him;
> the sea is his, for he made it,
> and the dry land which his hands fashioned.
>
> (Psalm 95.3–5)

Dawn found them skirting the treacherous waters off Bardsey, which had already claimed the lives of several pilgrims eager to reach this holy island. Founded many years earlier, the community welcomed a steady stream of people who dared cross the lethal tide races and whirlpools of the Sound. But on this occasion, with the tide slack and the wind moderate, all was well. The more they knew about the potential hazards of this voyage, the more miraculous their easy passage must have seemed.

For much of the second day, the little boat was out of sight of land. The customary round of offices, some bailing of water seeping in, and their frugal meal still gave them time to ponder the likely outcome of this strange undertaking, talking quietly among themselves or dozing in the sun in unaccustomed unemployment. Then, in the middle of the afternoon, high cliffs began to appear, broad sentinels pushed out into the sea, with white breakers at their feet. They altered course slightly, to reach around St David's Head, bastion of the Welsh churches. Closer in, they could make out the fertile fields on the cliff tops, while down by the water the spray of the breakers metamorphosed periodically into hurrying, wheeling gulls. St David's personal reputation as a strict moralist and ascetic was well known. His monks farmed without the aid of draught animals, pulling the ploughs themselves, and all property was strictly held in common. Even in David's old age, their diet was still frugal in the extreme; he ate bread and cabbage and drank only water, earning for himself the nickname 'aquaticus'. These extremes were not admired by all; some detected in it a touch of pharisaical pride. Worse still, it went with an egalitarianism that risked upsetting the already fragile social order. Gildas of Rhys, the recently deceased elder statesman of the British church, had had sharp words for those who took this attitude to extremes:

> They find fault with all the brothers who have not joined them in their presumptious practices. While they eat bread in prescribed measure, they boast of it without measure. While they drink water, they drink the cup of enmity. While they enjoy dry meals, they enjoy slanderous gossip with them ... they prefer slaves to masters, the common crowd to kings, lead to gold, iron to silver, the training stake to the vine. They prefer fasting to Christian love, vigils to justice, their own particular ideas to unity, the part to the whole church, strictness to humility and ultimately, man to God.[7]

All over south Wales this dispute rumbled on like distant summer thunder. The dozens of other monasteries that dotted the landscape, some large centres, others no more than tiny 'llans' named for their hermit-founders, were distributed at some point along the spectrum. Some followed David's extreme asceticism, others were more moderate, others were frankly rather lax and becoming more so with each year that passed.

Next to St David's Head, the curragh sailed past Ramsey Island, a pertinent reminder of the perils of misjudging the community mood. Justinian, its founder, had combined personal austerity with right-wing social opinions, taking over one of the many abandoned Roman estates and farming it with serfs. But common though this practice was, it had not worked for him. Either his asceticism, or his bad managerial skills, or perhaps the fact that he had spent many years living in Brittany, soon made him deeply unpopular, and he had recently been hacked to death by his labourers. Justinian now lay buried at Porthstinian on the mainland.

The precipitous cliffs of Ramsey, Skomer and Skokholm meanwhile were offering their age-old spectacular show to passing vessels, as thousands of seabirds dived and called and bobbed about the boat. Friendly, incongruous puffins, elegant guillemots, cormorants, razorbills, and glorious flashes of silver as gannets plunged head-long into the sea. All fishing and feeding their young, their noise followed downwind long after the islands were left behind.

Then south again, on the last leg of this present voyage, across open waters as darkness fell around them. The open mouth of the Bristol channel is exposed to the full force of the Atlantic swells, and a northerly wind makes it a daunting lee shore. Even today, with all the benefits of lighthouses, buoys and charts, those relying on wind or paddle alone find the West Country shores a formidable prospect, with miles of cliffs alternating with the pounding surf of the few beaches. It was this coastline that came into view at first light for Columbanus' party, after their second night at sea. The high point of Trevose Head jutted aggressively out, then the lower cliffs and, as they slipped gradually nearer, the long clear expanse of golden sand and creaming surf stretched below the grassy cliffs of Watergate Bay. Around the soft, brown little headland, the roar of the breakers was muted by the shelter of Towan Head, and there they came into the curving arms of the little bay, pulled up the boat safely above the falling tide, and unloaded their few possessions.

Notes

1 Jonas, 10 (Munro, 1895).
2 Pliny, *Natural History*, IV, 104 (Healy, 1991).
3 'Brendan' is now on display at Craggaunowen, Co. Clare.
4 Now on display at Kilmartin, Argyll.
5 *The 'Navigatio' of St Brendan the Abbot*, IV (eighth or ninth century) (Webb, 1983).
6 Bede's *Ecclesiastical History of the English People*, III.15 (731 AD) (McClure and Collins, 1994, 1999).
7 Gildas of Rhys, Fragments of Letters, 3 (Latin text in Winterbottom, 1978).

6

West Country Interlude

Long before Newquay became famous as a seaside resort, the whole of this part of North Cornwall bore the name of St Columb...

Both churches are supposed to be dedicated to St Columba but there is no written record of this. It is not even known who this St Columba was...[1]

If Columbanus was aiming for a distant land, why would he have landed in Cornwall? Why not sail on around Land's End and over to Brittany in a single passage? Actually, this line of reasoning misses part of the significance of his journey. Then, far more than now, to travel hopefully was more valuable than to arrive, and the destination was less important than the encounters along the way. With hindsight, it may look as though Columbanus was aiming for Brittany, but since that name was first used for Cornwall, and only later applied to the Armorican peninsular as it was settled by British emigrants, his intended destination, if he had one, is not clear.

By the time Columbanus reached Cornwall, he was already far from Bangor. When Columba of Iona went into 'voluntary exile' 25 years earlier, he had only to sail a third of the distance, to feel himself completely cut off from the ties of his past life. St Samson, who according to his *Life* was inspired to begin his travels by an angelic vision, did not go far at all to begin his 'exile'; even for such a rigorous enthusiast as him, the crossing from South Wales to Cornwall counted as a pilgrimage 'beyond the sea'.[2] In Cornwall, just as on Iona, Christianity was still knocking at the doors of the old pagan ways, and there was work in plenty to be done.

It was a rich land to which Columbanus had come. Fertile, blessed with a milder climate even than the Leinster of his childhood, it had since time immemorial supplied tin and copper ores to visiting traders, and been the route through which Irish gold was exported to Gaul. On the headlands and inland hilltops, ancient forts bore witness to the prestige of local rulers, and the reoccupation of some sites was a testimony to new patterns of power in the wake of Rome's collapse. One such fort guarded the eastern end of Newquay Bay, while inland, the mighty fortress of Castle-an-Dinas guarded the way over the moors to the Fowey estuary and France.

Along most of this coastline, the land rises abruptly from the scattered bays. But at Newquay there is a gentle two-mile walk up from the beach, to a place where the land makes a shoulder above the stream running down to Porth. A knoll hides the site from the bay itself; an ideal place to build a temporary encampment, with running water close by, the bay below, and a warm sheltered southerly aspect. Here, perhaps, Columbanus and his companions built huts from the materials ready to hand: oak, hazel and rushes. Here, certainly, in later years, a church was dedicated to an unknown 'St Columba'. A mediaeval legend[3] told how this person was an Irish virgin princess, pursued to Cornwall by an ardent pagan suitor who chased her up the valley and cut off her head near Ruthvoes, whence a stream still flows down to the sea. No one will deny that this story is more romantic than a dedication to an Irish monk, one of dozens pausing for a while before moving on to Brittany. But the fable lacks antiquity, and even as it was recorded doubts were expressed about its authenticity.

As in Ireland and Wales, so too here the landscape was dotted with religious foundations large and small. St Mawgan, St Ervan and St Merryn had all lived and died in the immediate hinterland of Watergate Bay. Further up the coast, on the Padstow estuary, and over as far as Bodmin, were a series of communities of St Petroc, a Welshman who had probably visited Ireland before going to Cornwall. And the saintly Irish Abbess Issey, who died about the time Columbanus went to Bangor, had a nephew Dagan who came over to be a disciple of Petroc, and founded a community near Padstow, dedicated to his aunt. St Samson too came this way; from Wales he landed in the Camel estuary and made contact with the monastery of Docco (now St Kew). But Samson, unlike many others, did not stay long. Distressed by the lax standards at Docco, and violently at odds with the pagan beliefs of many Cornish people, he crossed Bodmin Moor to the Fowey estuary. There, he settled for a while in a hermitage before taking ship to Brittany.

Perhaps it was the sheer concentration of Irish and Welsh monasteries in this narrow northern coastal strip that encouraged Columbanus to move on. At first, maybe some local sub-Roman aristocrat at Castle-an-Dinas granted him land on the site now linked with the legend of the virgin St Columba, at St Columb Major, and he stayed there long enough for hazy memories of his name to be preserved. Further inland, there were still flourishing pagan remnants, and the near presence of a group of foreign holy men might do much to boost the morale of a beleaguered Christian settlement.

But from the Newquay area Columbanus and his companions would soon hear about the ancient trade route up the River Camel and over the narrow watershed to the Fowey. They would hear about the many 'saints' who had travelled that way in the last few decades: Samson, Gildas, Brioc, Cadoc, Paul and Malo, to name but a few. Cornwall began to feel more like a transit camp than a destination, a point of departure for the lands beyond. So, taking their few possessions, they set out on the day-long walk to the Fowey, over the edge of the moor, beside lush pastures and along the steep-sided wooded valleys, down to the tidal estuary where Samson had once had a hermitage. There, they waited until they found a ship to carry them over to Brittany.

To even begin to understand these early travellers, one should approach Brittany from the sea. A small boat such as theirs would be best, relying on wind and oar alone, but failing that a commercial sailing to St Malo or Roscoff will do. One needs time to shake off some of the preconceptions of twenty-first-century Britain, and perhaps a touch of sea-sickness to induce a feeling of humility.

On a clear day, the south coast of England remains in view for hours, and it has not long finally melted over the horizon before one begins to imagine there may be land ahead. The tides become ever stronger, and eventually first Guernsey and then Jersey loom up.

The north-west shore of Guernsey, inhospitable and reef-fringed, gives way to the straight western shore of Jersey, its long expanse of sand visible between the red cliffs. Behind the islands is the long, long line of the Normandy coast, and to the south the straining eyes can pick out the low Isles de Chausey and the Breton shore. Now the attention is more focused, as details of the land ahead begin to emerge. Far over to the left, a huge bay stretches into the distance, uninviting and slightly sinister. Well might Columbanus and his crew pray to escape being drawn down into it by the currents, for they had no hope of beating off such a lee shore. Closer to hand, the peninsula of alternating red rocky headlands and sandy coves offered them a more inviting landing, and wind and tide deposited them ashore on a long beach between rounded islets, the pale sand shelving gradually away into the sea as the boat grounded gently on the sheltered tide line.

Hauling the boat up the beach a little and looking around, the group would have appreciated the immense good fortune that brought them to land at just that point. For the bay where they landed has no cliffs at its head, but is backed by sand-dunes, fringed with trees and heavy all summer with the scent of broom. Over it all thrilled the glorious, bubbling, liquid laughter of the larks; their own little brown bird, the 'lithe little lark', dearest companion of the Irish hermitage, welcoming them to France. With what additional fervour did they say the office, and what new meaning did they vow always to attach to that ancient question: 'Who is this, that even the wind and the waves obey him?'

This traditional landing site of Columbanus is still remembered. Set back among the potato fields behind the car park and the dunes in a bay just east of St Malo, a wonderfully simple grey stone cross was put up in 1892, in place of an earlier one that had crumbled half away. At its foot, a polished granite tablet reads in French:

Calvary erected in 1892 in the place
where according to tradition
St Columban landed to begin
evangelizing this country.

Notes

1 *A Brief History of St Columb Minor Parish Church.*
2 *The Life of St Samson*, 45 (seventh century) (Taylor, 1925).
3 Collected by Nicholas Roscarrock, *c.* 1610, from a legend in Cornish.

7
Around Brittany

Here they rested for a while to recover their strength and dis-
cussed their plans anxiously . . . in order to remain longer if they
found they could sow the seeds of salvation; or in case they
found the hearts of the people in darkness, go on to the nearest
nations.[1]

Jonas did his research for his *Life of Columbanus* faithfully, speaking to many people who had known the saint personally. But there
is no record of Jonas travelling any further west than Meaux, near
Paris, and by the time he went there Columbanus had been dead
nearly 40 years. So the brief mention of the stay in Brittany needs
to be treated with caution. Did Columbanus hope to settle there,
as so many had done before, or were his thoughts on a more remote
exile, to the east?

As a foreign land, Brittany was not much more exotic to
Columbanus than Cornwall. Even today, with its characteristic
Frenchness, it is not difficult to see how similar it is to the West
Country or the Channel Islands. Fifteen centuries ago, it was more
similar still. Like the West Country, Brittany had been on the
fringes of the Roman world; both were now witnessing the tide
of Germanic migrations engulfing their neighbours, and both had
received their share of refugees as a result. The plagues which
swept up across Gaul and into Britain between 540 and 550 had
further encouraged emigration to Brittany, which had for some
reason escaped the worst of the disease. First and second generation immigrants from Britain were on every side. By Columbanus'
day, Latin had been largely replaced by Celtic again, and although
the Roman cities survived, the place names with their tre-,
plou- and lan- prefixes were unmistakably Celtic, as was the people's

determination not to be bullied by their larger neighbours.

The numerous villages, headlands and hills dedicated to particular saints tell the story of the sub-Roman church and its people. Over 200 of these 'saints' crossed to Brittany from Britain, along with thousands of other people. As in the West Country, many of these saints are mainly commemorated within a small geographical area, perpetuating the memory of their sphere of influence. Church dedications and place names relating to Columbanus are found in two distinct clusters in Brittany, one on the north-east coast, and one on the south. The pattern is sufficiently clear-cut to suggest at least the possibility that it relates to the areas in which he was active.

Just inland from the bay where they first landed, in a slight hollow of the gently rolling hills, a place not unlike St Columb Minor, lies the village of St Coulomb, the scene perhaps of those earliest days in Brittany. Columbanus is remembered in the village with a statue and a window in the church. Maybe the local ruler, Count Judael, made the Irishmen a small grant of land for their new settlement. South of St Coulomb, the little party would have found a land of dense forest, some virgin wildwood but much of it old farmland returning to wilderness because there were no longer enough men to plough it. The 'barbarian' invasions and the plagues had halved the population of Gaul and here on the borders of Frankish territory the pillage and famine must have been terrible.

Nearby in this forest a second settlement may have been founded, or a grant of land made, but all trace of it has now vanished except for the name of 'the marsh of St Colomb' and a nearby hill which also bears his name. For, sometime in the next hundred years, the whole low-lying coastal forest was swamped by the sea, cutting off the hill of Mont St Michel, isolating the nearby Mt Dol in a marsh and leaving the salt water lapping at the edge of the hill of Dol de Bretagne. Only in the thirteenth century did the slow process of reclaiming the polder-lands get under way, as population pressure increased.

It was in Dol that Samson had settled after he came to Brittany, and there he had founded a monastery and acted as bishop for the previous Count, Judael's father. In Dol, Samson had eventually died, some 25 years before Columbanus arrived, and already his cult had become widespread. Dol was one of the most powerful of the great British foundations in Brittany, and Samson was as famous as his see; there are villages far and wide named after him, all the way to Finistère. To Dol Columbanus may have come soon after his arrival, to pay his respects to the abbot (probably by then St Genevé) and to learn about the local situation.

There were other, more recently established expatriate communities in the immediate vicinity, too. On an island in the mouth of the River Rance lived St Malo, a fiery and impetuous Welshman. Consecrated bishop with the support of Samson and the Count, he was a complex and colourful character. Much given to riding round his estates roaring out psalms at the top of his voice, he took good care that the serfs were fairly treated. But he was always eager to add to the wealth of his monastic lands, and later arrivals tended to move away to make their own foundations: men like St Sulian, a prince of Powys, who visited Malo on his arrival in Brittany but soon moved upstream ten kilometres to settle where the Priory of St Suliac now stands. Malo and Columbanus seem to have got on well enough together: according to some sources, Malo later travelled across France to visit Columbanus in the Vosges.[2]

Columbanus and his little group of followers seem to have moved about this area of northern Brittany, perhaps looking for somewhere suitable to settle. There are three villages that may be associated with them. Near St Brieuc, Plouvenez-Quintin has an ancient chapel of Columban, a holy well, and a traditional feast day or 'pardon' in his honour, as well as some relics; further west again, Brelidy also has relics, a holy well and two pardons, one in the summer, but one on 21 November, which is given in some manuscripts as the day of Columbanus' death. Thirdly, at Lanmeur ('the great monastery' in Breton) there is a church whose origins are lost in the past. Previously dedicated to Columban, a building here was destroyed in a ninth-century Norman raid and only its crypt remains.

Unlike the expatriate English of the nineteenth century, Columbanus and his contemporaries were not gregarious. They were intent on finding their own private piece of wilderness, their own desert. But as they moved west along the red granite coast, they had no sooner left the vicinity of Ploumanach ('the people of the monk'), where the Irishman Guirec laboured, than they came into the orbit of St Pol de Leon, a thriving Welsh foundation. So maybe they abandoned the idea of settling on the north coast, and turned south, travelling perhaps by the old Roman road from Dol to Rennes and then on either by road or boat down the River Vilaine to the coast.

That journey must have been a heart-rending experience. The Vilaine marked the border between Brittany and the more securely held Frankish lands beyond. For all that Bishop Gregory of Tours, writing in 590, said confidently that 'From the days of King Clovis [who died in 511], the Bretons were under the dominion of the Franks and their rulers were called counts not kings',[3] the Bretons clearly thought otherwise. Gregory himself admits that in 578, 579, 585, 586, 588 *and* 589 there were major border incursions: 'They stole the wine-harvest, destroyed the cultivated fields and carried off as slaves those who lived on the country estates'.[4] The landscape Columbanus and his little company were now crossing bore the scars of these frequent raids. The repeated attacks on the precious vines, right at the northern limits of their range and yet so vital to church life, and the regular destruction of the crops in the fields, must have depressed the farmers beyond measure. The loss of manpower as one side or the other took prisoners and slaves, and the terrible hardship caused when the villages were burnt, made sustained agriculture all but impossible. Nor was it only the serfs, away from the relative safety of the city walls, who felt the trauma of the times. Gregory tells a sad story of the daughter of the bishop of Rennes, murdered in cold blood by a Frankish courtier in a dispute over the ownership of a vineyard.

The city of Vannes was ruled over, Roman style, by a bishop appointed by the Franks, but its ownership was hotly disputed by the Bretons. It was the scene of major fighting in 589, and the role of the clergy was more than a little ambiguous. Bishop Regalis felt sufficiently unsure of his reception by his nominal overlords to send a deputation to meet the approaching Frankish general and assure him of the city's loyalty. His delicate balancing act, attempting to save his city from yet more pillage, must have caused him many anxious moments: 'Bishop Regalis swore an oath, and so did his clergy and his townsfolk. "We have nothing whatsoever to reproach ourselves with in our relations with our lords and masters," he said, "nor have we ever been foolish enough to do anything to their disadvantage. We have to do as the Bretons tell us, and this irks us very much".[5]

It is hard, looking now at the fertile farmland and dense woods that surround Vannes, to believe that in the Middle Ages this was mostly bleak, exhausted moorland, or that in Columbanus' day the Roman settlements and estates were slowly being engulfed by the forests and weeds, just as their civilization was vanishing in continuous petty warfare. Just down the coast from Vannes, though, on a wild and windy granite promontory, was a sight that must have rejoiced Columbanus' heart. Here Gildas, who in Columbanus' youth had travelled to Ireland to advise the monastic leaders there, whom the young Columbanus may have met and whom he certainly admired, and who was known in the Celtic churches as 'Gildas the Wise', had founded a monastery when he himself was only a young man. Some said it was on his return from a pilgrimage to Rome. After an active life in Wales, Gildas had returned to his own corner of Brittany, where he died in about 570. Columbanus much later quoted Gildas as an authority to Pope Gregory the Great. He would have surely seized this opportunity to visit his monastery and pray at the wise man's tomb.

From this dramatic site, now known as St Gildas de Rhys, Columbanus may have been drawn to pay a visit to the stone 'alignments' of Carnac: nearly 4,000 menhirs in three groups of parallel lines, 20 kilometres away across the relative shelter of the Bay of Quiberon. In those days, Quiberon was an island, not yet joined to Plouharnel by its long isthmus of sand dunes, but still it would have broken the worst of the Atlantic swell. A convenient landing site, just west of Carnac, is still known as Pointe St Colomban, and the nearby peninsular carries the same name. A well and a church just west of the modern town are dedicated to Columbanus, along the Rue St Columban. While they were there they might have developed a taste for mussels and oysters (farmed here avidly in the Roman era), for seafood would have been more readily available than bread in those troubled times.

But Columbanus would not have visited the alignments to marvel at the ingenuity of the people who erected them, or to wonder and produce fantastic theories of what they represent. For him, and for scores of vigorous and uncompromising saints of his time, these menhirs were a focus of pagan customs and beliefs, much of it still all too alive. Today we may see these ancient peoples as part of our ancestry, and yearn to understand more about their lives, but for Columbanus and his contemporaries their beliefs were an evil power to be overcome.

All along this coastal region are menhirs, some huge standing stones over ten metres high, many smaller but clustered into groups. There had been signs of the pagan past in Ireland, and more in Cornwall, but here it was impossible to miss them, and the hold of Christianity on the minds of the people was less secure. Should Columbanus dedicate his life to rooting out the pagan religion of the Bretons? Or was the already large number of British settlers a disincentive, even here on the south coast. For here, too, he found he was not first; St Cadoc had worked near Carnac, St Ronan on the far west coast, and there was a large new foundation on the exposed cliffs of Pointe de Mathieu, to name but a few. As they travelled around, he had time to revolve in his mind the question of where they should go. Should they rise to the challenge of the paganism that was still so evident, and do battle with the darkness of the land, or should they move on from the near presence of all these countrymen, and find a space of their own where they could settle in peace and establish a corner of heaven on earth through the labour of their mutual society?

There are Breton traditions that Columbanus did travel west along the south coast, as he had done in the north, this time along the Roman 'trunk road' from Vannes towards Brest. At Quimperlé, the eleventh-century abbey of Ste Croix is on the site of a much earlier monastery, founded perhaps by St Gurthiern of Wales; ruins nearby are dedicated to Columban. Further west again, past the beautiful beech and oak woods that clothe the red sandstone hills, and into the higher land beyond, lies Kernevel. Now a small village, it boasts a large sixteenth-century church, recently rebuilt, and a statue and stained-glass window of Columbanus, and used to celebrate its pardon with a procession of relics on the third Sunday of November – the Sunday nearest to the date of his death.

They may for a while have considered finding an isolated place away from the Breton coast. Central Brittany is a large, relatively wild area even today. The Romans had never civilized it and it remained dense forest long after the coastal strip was divided up into rich estates. No cities existed there, and few saints and settlers had braved it since. North of Vannes, the town of Locmenec'h ('the place of the monks') has an abbey reputed to have been founded as a result of a visit by Columbanus. But it, like Malansac, 45 kilometres to the south-west, may equally well have been founded by Columbanus' followers, much later. It is unlikely that anyone will ever know, for here too there was a devastating Norman raid and the church was not rebuilt until the seventeenth century. Certainly the influence of Columbanus continued to be felt in southern Brittany for many years: at Quimper there was a double monastery under the Columbanian Rule as late as the eleventh century.

So what was it that finally decided Columbanus to leave Brittany and cross over into Frankish territory? He had stayed long enough to leave a lasting mark on the Breton folk memory, even in those days of multitudinous saints. But perhaps he was less popular with their rulers. Both Samson and Gildas, in whose footsteps he was following, were men noted for their vigour, denouncing backsliding and laxity wherever they saw it. But they had both settled in the Frankish borderlands; perhaps among the majority of the Bretons, condemnation of the old religion was not so acceptable, and Columbanus had fallen foul of the local hierarchy. Is this the origin of Jonas' cryptic remark about the minds of the people being in darkness? If so, Columbanus would not have left with his tail between his legs. He carried with him the memory of the people he had left behind, longing to return and lead them into the light. Maybe this is the better explanation for the foundations at Malansac and Locmenec'h: the fulfilment of a promise to return to the help of the Bretons; communities established in the troubled border area, where they could be of most comfort, as soon as he had the means.

Or perhaps after a year or two travelling around exploring, seeking a niche where he could settle, he had come to the conclusion that this was just not the place he was meant to be. Brittany was, as he had discovered, already well supplied with evangelists and monasteries, but few had crossed the border regions into France proper, and there, he would have heard from his Breton friends, there was ample scope for setting an example of Christian living.

A third possibility is that, with the first generation of saints mostly dead, and the first great wave of immigration already half a century old, the British communities were becoming less zealous. Of the great early 'names' of Brittany, only Malo was still alive; he lived on, ruling his various communities in his own inimitable way until his death in 621. But other communities must have relaxed as the first generation of leadership died, and Columbanus may not have found this a comfortable fact to live with, or they with him. When Bishop Samson had wanted to stay in Cornwall half a century earlier, the local abbot straightaway began to feel uncomfortable:

> 'O most loving father, the journey thou hast undertaken is a thing to be desired by a servant of God, for God in the gospel praises him who becomes a pilgrim for his sake: nevertheless the thing that thou askest, that thou mightest stay with us, is not convenient . . . for I wish you to know this, that we come short of our former practice.' Now when St Samson heard these things, he was astonished at his doctrine . . .[6]

Whatever the reason, when Columbanus had been in Brittany for a year or two, he turned his face to the east, crossed the River Vilaine, and entered France.

Notes

1 Jonas, 10 (Munro, 1895).
2 *The Life of St Malo* is lost, but it has been partially reconstructed from references in other documents.
3 Gregory of Tours, *History of the Franks*, IV.4 (590 AD) (Thorpe, 1974).
4 Gregory of Tours, *History of the Franks*, IX.24 (Thorpe, 1974).
5 Gregory of Tours, *History of the Franks*, X.9 (Thorpe, 1974).
6 *The Life of Samson*, 46 (Taylor, 1925).

8

Into France

Accordingly, they left Brittany and proceeded into the Gallic lands. At that time, either because of the numerous enemies from without, or on account of the carelessness of the bishops, the Christian faith had almost departed from that country... Everywhere that he went the noble man preached the Gospel. And it pleased the people because his teaching was adorned with eloquence and enforced by examples of virtue.[1]

The lands Columbanus entered were indeed not happy. Duke Ebrachar, whom the king had put in charge of the Breton borders, was neither wise nor just. While attempting to put down the 589 Breton uprisings, he had allowed his army to ravage the Frankish countryside for miles around, so that on his return to court he was obliged to find an alternative route, for fear of reprisals from his own countrymen. He took the opportunity of fresh pastures thus presented to pillage the city of Tours as well. The king was furious, 'reproached him bitterly and ordered him to leave his presence.'[2]

Jonas may have been overstating the moral decay of the church, but the last 200 years in Gaul had not been easy. Although there were over a hundred dioceses, many with a proud and faithful history, the bishops and their clergy had been forced by circumstance to undertake much of the civil administration as the structures of Roman society collapsed in the face of the barbarian invasions. Some had coped well, organizing famine relief, negotiating with the invaders, founding churches and monasteries and carrying on with their pastoral work. But for others it was all too much and bishops became magnates, or drunkards, or fell into the pockets of the warlords. When Clovis, King of the Franks, was baptized in 496, things improved marginally, but attitudes do not change

The Frankish Kingdoms in the days of Columbanus

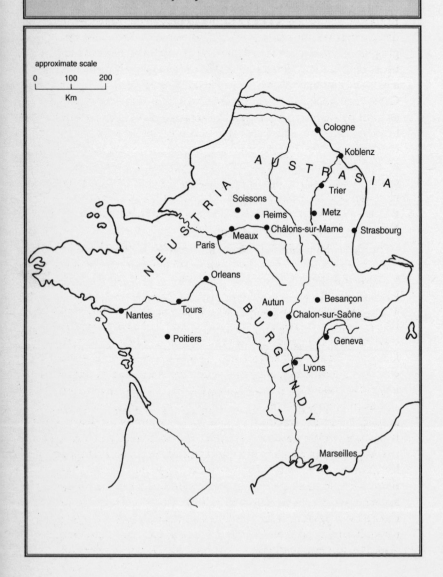

approximate scale

0   100   200

Km

Cologne

Koblenz

AUSTRASIA

Trier

Soissons

Reims   Metz

Châlons-sur-Marne   Strasbourg

Meaux

NEUSTRIA   Paris

Orleans

Autun   Besançon

Nantes   Tours   Chalon-sur-Saône

BURGUNDY   Geneva

Poitiers

Lyons

Marseilles

overnight and the century that followed was one long sorry tale of internecine strife, simony and assaults on clergy and churches alike.

In 561, the Frankish lands, which by then stretched from Brittany to Nuremberg and from the Rhone to the Rhine, were divided between the four surviving grandsons of Clovis. One was grasping and mean, one so bad that Gregory of Tours summed him up as 'the Nero and Herod of our time', one was merely mediocre, and one, Guntram, was on the whole quite good. Fortunately for Gaul, 'good King Guntram' who was 'well known for his charity and much given to vigils and fasting'³ outlived all his less desirable brothers and where an heir survived he was willing to act as regent or adviser until the boy grew up. Thus it was that when Columbanus arrived in France, Guntram ruled uncontested in Burgundy, with capital cities at Orleans and Chalon-sur-Saône, was adviser to his nephew Childebert, King of Austrasia in the Rhinelands, and was regent for the six-year-old Lothar, King of Neustria in present-day Normandy.

If the political situation was temporarily stable, the royal family and church leaders could not be relied upon to set a good example of behaviour. In 590, a convent at Tours was stripped of all its possessions by the estranged daughter of the founder, who then assembled a gang of ruffians to steal all the produce of its estates. In the same year, there was a national scandal centred on the convent of the Holy Cross at Poitiers; a violent revolt broke out, led by the Princess Clothild, in which an armed mob stormed the church, the abbess and prioress were assaulted and accusations of immorality and misconduct flew on all sides.

Into this environment came the band of Irishmen, moving around, preaching wherever they could, living largely on charity. It seems that Columbanus was all this time feeling his way into a new vocation, not only as a preacher and teacher, but as the strong leader of his group, with distinctive ideas of how a Christian community should be shaped. Once they had settled down, he would assemble his ideas in his collection of Rules. For now, it seems from the pages of Jonas as if he was formulating the key points in his mind, observing what really mattered in close-knit communal life. The days at sea would have taught him, in a way that weeks on

The early Merovingian Kings of France (with regnal dates and principal capital cities)

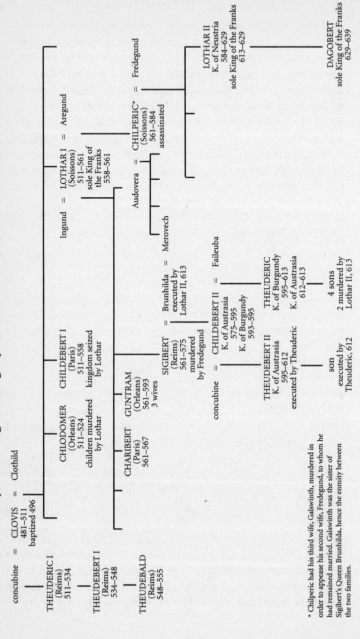

concubine = CLOVIS = Clothild
481–511
baptized 496

THEUDERIC I
(Reims)
511–534

THEUDEBERT I
(Reims)
534–548

THEUDEBALD
548–555

CHLODOMER
(Orleans)
511–524
children murdered
by Lothar

CHILDEBERT I
(Paris)
511–558
kingdom seized
by Lothar

Ingund = LOTHAR I = Aregund
(Soissons)
511–561
sole King of
the Franks
558–561

= Fredegund

CHARIBERT
(Paris)
561–567

GUNTRAM
(Orleans)
561–593
3 wives

SIGIBERT
(Reims)
561–575
murdered
by Fredegund

= Brunhilda = Merovech
executed by
Lothar II, 613

Audovera = CHILPERIC*
(Soissons)
561–584
assassinated

LOTHAR II
K. of Neustria
584–629
sole King of the Franks
613–629

CHILDEBERT II
K. of Austrasia
575–595
K. of Burgundy
593–595

= Faileuba

DAGOBERT
sole King of the Franks
629–639

concubine =

THEUDEBERT II
K. of Austrasia
595–612
executed by Theuderic

THEUDERIC
K. of Burgundy
595–613
K. of Austrasia
612–613

son
executed by
Theuderic, 612

4 sons
2 murdered by
Lothar II, 613

* Chilperic had his third wife, Galswinth, murdered in
order to appease his second wife, Fredegund, to whom he
had remained married. Galswinth was the sister of
Sigibert's Queen Brunhilda, hence the enmity between
the two families.

land could not, the need for absolute obedience to a superior, subordination of the individual to the collective good, and the value of good humour. Even the best of voyages has its moments of tension and drama, not least for them the times of waiting for their frail craft to beach on the unfamiliar lee shores. And now these months of travelling around together would have tested their resolve, searched out the weaknesses in their unity, highlighted the petty irritations.

The spirit of the final Rules is plain to see in Jonas' description of their early days in France. The emphasis on humility and self-offering love is reflected in Rule 9 and in the opening sentence:

> Let a monk live in a monastery under the discipline of one father and in fellowship with many, so that from one he may learn humility, and from another patience ... First of all we are taught 'to love God with our whole heart, our whole mind and our whole strength and our neighbours as ourselves';

Simple words, maybe, but not so easy to fulfil. The desire to punish embryonic pride severely is also conspicuous: 'Let him who does not ask pardon when corrected do penance with a prolonged fast', and 'Let no grand word proceed, then, from a monk's mouth lest his own grand work perish.'[4]

Most of all, Columbanus was realizing the dangers of idle, negative talk in a small community; how fast it can destroy trust and the bonds that unite people. In Rule 2, he later wrote with feeling:

> They will be rightly condemned who refused to say just things when they could, but preferred in a prattling profusion of words to utter what is evil, unjust, ungodly, empty, harmful, untrustworthy, untrue, contentious, abusive, filthy, fictitious, blasphemous, rude and devious. We must therefore be silent on these and suchlike matters and speak with discretion and judgement so that neither slanders nor violent counter-arguments break out in a vicious excess of talk.

Of the little company now living in Gaul, Jonas says, 'No one dared return evil for evil, or let fall a harsh word; so that people must have believed that an angelic life was being lived by mortal men.'[5]

Did Jonas know that Comgall's Bangor was known as 'The Valley of Angels'? Or was this a spontaneous tribute to Columbanus himself? The group made quite a stir in western France, and were not there very long before an unexpected summons came to move Columbanus still further on his pilgrimage.

Notes

1 Jonas, 11 (Munro, 1895).
2 Gregory of Tours, *The History of the Franks*, X.9 (Thorpe, 1974).
3 Gregory of Tours, *The History of the Franks*, IX.21 (Thorpe, 1974).
4 Columbanus' Communal Rule 8; Columbanus' Monastic Rule 5 (*c.* 600 AD).
5 Jonas, 11 (Munro, 1895).

PART III

The Eagle in Flight

9
To the Frankish Court

Finally, the reports about Columbanus spread to the court... When the holy man with his companions appeared before the king, the greatness of his learning caused him to stand high in the favour of the king[1] and court.[2]

It is not surprising that reports about Columbanus should have reached the court. Not, that is, because of the presence of foreign nationals on Frankish soil: borders hardly existed then in the way they do now, or even as they had done in the Western Empire of Rome, when population movements were to some extent controlled. Brittany felt strong ties of kin and culture to western Britain; France thought it owned Brittany. So to move from one to the other was to move along a gradient rather than through a series of borders. It is far more likely that attention was drawn to him by the novelty of his teaching style and his mode of living. Just like his kindred soul Francis of Assisi hundreds of years later, Columbanus took literally the biblical injunctions on poverty and humility and the command to 'give up father and mother, wife and children, brothers and sisters, for my sake'. And just as Francis was to find all those centuries later, Columbanus must have discovered that this disturbed some people, not least the bishops and other clergy whose 'patch' he was trampling on. Probably news of these strangely religious men reached the ears of one of these bishops, of Rennes, Nantes or Angers, and so was passed on to the king. They do not seem to have ruffled feathers in Tours, or at least if they did, Bishop Gregory did not see fit to report it in his *History*, which is a shame. It would throw a fascinating sidelight on Columbanus to hear what the perceptive Gregory thought of him.

Royal messengers were sent out, found Columbanus and

summoned him to court. How they tracked him down is not recorded, but Gaul was a civilized place, in spite of having fallen on hard times. Much of its old network of Roman roads with their inns and posthouses was still in use, and the cities with their bishops served as nodes for the transmission of information. Out in the countryside, the population was sparse and brigands all too common, but it was not a completely desperate situation. There were churches in plenty, and many of the wealthier estates were efficiently farmed by a new generation of Frankish aristocracy keen to generate a new urbane image and make France their own. Reports of Columbanus' whereabouts and the latest stories about his preaching and extraordinary lifestyle would be hot news.

The monks seem to have accepted the summons to court without demur. Perhaps it would reveal to Columbanus his life's work. Little chance of martyrdom, for which the Irish secretly yearned, but perhaps an opportunity to do other great things, as yet undreamed of. His mother's story of the days before his birth came back to him; her vision of the sun shining out from her and shedding light on the dark world around. Was this the time when that vision would be fulfilled?

Escorted by the royal messengers, they walked up the huge road beside the Loire. Sometimes on the floodbanks, directly overlooking the unbelievably wide river and its busy craft, sometimes away from the banks where the road negotiated a swamp or a confluence, they went on until they approached Tours. The name itself thrilled them. In the huge city, over on the long peninsula of land where two rivers joined, was the newly restored cathedral, rededicated in 580. Several other churches and much of the city had been damaged in recent fires and these, too, were being rebuilt. But far more precious, just outside the city walls stood the great church of St Martin, a hundred years old and restored in the last few decades with the help of a generous royal donation. It was larger than any church Columbanus had ever seen or imagined. Larger even than the feasting halls of Irish kings, it was 60 paces long and 20 paces wide, the brightly coloured, newly painted walls of the nave rising up high into the roof vaulting. In the central shrine, St Martin's body lay in its marble-topped tomb, the focus of pilgrimage and prayer for nearly 200 years. Around it were the tombs of 14 other bishops who had occupied the see since Martin. They had been buried here rather than in their cathedral, a testimony to the power of the man and his marvels.

After visiting the tomb to pray, they would have returned to the north bank of the river. There, squeezed between the river and the cliffs behind, where a school stands today, was the monastery of Marmoutier, St Martin's own foundation and his retreat from the burdens of episcopal duties and city life. For Martin, like the Irish, was a country man, more interested in building up the rural church than the dignity his office demanded. But, like most hermits before and since, he was soon inundated with visitors, wanting to share his solitude, wanting to experience it, to learn from him, or merely to interview him. People flocked there from all over the world, from Italy, from Africa and from the Middle East, to sit at Martin's feet. Most important of all for Columbanus, St Ninian himself was believed to have come here, shortly before Martin's death, on his way back from Rome. Taking inspiration from what he found here, he had journeyed on, to found the school and monastery at Whithorn, the wellspring that had nourished the early north Irish church. When Ninian visited, there were already about 80 monks at Marmoutier, living in separate cells, some simple huts, 'but most of them had hollowed out shelters for themselves in the rock of the overhanging mountain'.[3] The numerous caves hollowed out in the sheer white cliff behind the school are clearly visible even today, some still in use as cellars. Martin's monks spent most of their time in prayer alone, but they also shared a communal life, a pattern which was widely admired and imitated. Many of the nobility were attracted there, and Marmoutier soon became a source of bishops and church leaders for much of Gaul, for 'what kind of city or church would it be that did not covet a bishop from Martin's monastery?'[4]

Leaving this place of hallowed memories behind them, Columbanus' party continued on their way up the river. Talking to their Frankish guides was not easy, their only common languages the fragmentary Latin the Franks knew and the rudimentary Frankish that Gall, the linguist among them, had managed to pick up. If the king had sent a cleric with a good command of Latin as

part of the escort, he would have been able to interpret for them.
Preaching to the peasants of France would have been much easier;
in western districts the Celtic languages may still have lingered,
while 500 years of close contact with Rome had left a strongly
Latin-influenced population, speaking a peculiar but recognizable
'Gallo-Roman', not yet fully adopted by the Germanic Franks and
eventually destined to evolve into modern French.

There was no particular rush on this journey, but a summons
from a king should not be treated lightly. So they made good
time, along the banks of the graceful river, still wider than they
imagined possible. The road surface was mostly still intact, and
along the way were occasional reminders of the Roman past: rows
of ornate tombs lining the road, or a shrine to the old gods at a
ford or a crossroads. At regular intervals were the imperial posting
stations, many falling into ruins but some converted to public inns
and eating houses, for this route pre-dated the Romans and had
outlived them. It was one of the great trade arteries of Europe, part
of a chain combining river and land transport that connected the
Mediterranean to Biscay and the Channel. For thousands of years
it had been brisk with trade; amber and flint, then iron goods,
later still amphorae of wine, spices, tin, gold, newly minted coins
for soldiers' pay, taxes, shellfish, salt, cereals and glassware, flowing
in both directions and much of it still flowing long after the heart
of Rome had ceased to beat. And all the time it had been a channel
for ideas: new techniques, new peoples, new religions, new invasions.
And up this same road came Columbanus, harbinger of more
innovations, marvelling at what he saw, walking ever eastward.

Four days' journeying brought them to Orleans, a major Roman
city like Tours, guarding a crucial bridging point of the Loire. It
stood at a point where roads met, where the traffic with the Channel
ports came down from the Seine to meet the Loire routes. Thirty
years earlier, King Guntram had chosen it as his principal capital
city, but now he spent more time at Chalon-sur-Saône, 300 kilometres further east. So they continued along the great road, which
turned south at Orleans along the winding course of the river.
For a further 150 kilometres they followed the Loire upstream,
through fertile rolling farmland and past seemingly endless forests,

past small settlements that faced the river and plied their trade on its waters. All the way up to Nevers, the Loire is still navigable today with care, in spite of modern extraction of water and its abandonment as a transport route. In the sixth century, it was deeper and busier by far, with convoys of flat-bottomed barges and punts, under sail, or towed or poled.

At Nevers, they finally left the valley, and struck off east again on another, smaller road, up through steeper hills and over the crest of the watershed to drop down into Autun, the last city before Chalon. Even 600 years after its foundation by the Emperor Augustus, Autun was something of a 'new town', built by the River Arroux as a civilized lowland capital for the local Aedui tribe, to replace their old hill fort of Bibracte up to the west. Entering the city from the west, one crossed the river on an imposing bridge, and came under a monumental, marble-faced gate leading to the broad main street. Wheeled traffic rumbled through the central arch, while the numerous pedestrians used two side-passages. Autun was an important road junction. Here the route over the watershed from the Loire to the Saône crossed another one going diagonally along the high ground, from Mâcon to Sens, and converged with the road from Decize and the upper Loire. As if to emphasize its strategic importance, a city milestone grandly gave directions for Rome and the Rhine. Although it was not large by Roman standards (1,000 by 1,250 metres), it must have been an impressive sight for Columbanus and his party, with its ancient walls still intact. Even the pavements were grand, wide enough for four men to walk abreast.

After Autun, two short days' walk was all that lay between them and Chalon. Down into the valley of the Dheune, then up over the final watershed and down again on the old road into Chalon, on a huge bend in the broad River Saône. Two days in which to think about the coming interview with the king. Why did he want to see them? What did he want of them? What would he be like? If they had met Bishop Gregory of Tours they might have received an encouraging report. King Guntram had a reputation for regular charitable giving, and had once ordered prayers and fasting when the plague was ravaging the country. On the other hand, he had inherited the Merovingian quick temper and his private life left something to be desired. After taking a mistress, he abandoned her to marry a lady who proceeded to murder his son, so he divorced her. He then married again, but chose no better; his second wife compelled him to swear to have her doctors killed if they could not cure her, and he duly did so. After this, he opted to remain a widower. If he took against a man, then woe betide him; he had had his chamberlain stoned to death on the mistaken suspicion that he had been poaching royal cattle, and Bishop Theodore of Marseilles was flung into prison for giving succour to a potential usurper. But the king was generally fair in his dealings with the church, appointing good bishops where he could, dismissing or exiling some of the bad ones, and calling councils to settle the more serious abuses he recognized. This complex character was the man whom Columbanus was about to meet. Now aged about 60, he had survived on his throne for almost 30 years, to become the most powerful ruler in northern Europe.

What did King Guntram see, as they were ushered into his presence? A strange-looking group of men, with the front part of their hair shaved and the back worn long so it fell to their shoulders. A group strangely evocative of St Martin and his first followers, with their odd garments, burning faith and meagre possessions, in striking contrast to the brightly dressed and bejewelled courtiers. But unlike Martin, Columbanus insisted that his followers were clean and relatively neat; he already had a reputation for punishing anyone who attended communion with unwashed hands.

So they talked, and the extent of Columbanus' learning struck the king from the moment he opened his mouth. For Columbanus was fluent in pure, classical Latin (even if he did speak with an Irish intonation), not the degraded Gallo-Roman that was on its way to becoming Old French, which the Franks were adopting. And he was familiar not just with the Bible, which he quoted effortlessly, but with several of the classical authors, too. He was an admirer of poetry, and did not feel it incompatible with his austerity that he wrote a little himself, in a variety of styles. He probably did not speak Greek, but may have had some knowledge of it from his days in the schoolrooms of Ireland. He was an experienced and gifted teacher, and a natural if stern leader of men. Small wonder that King Guntram was startled at this paragon of virtues and his ready-made nucleus of followers descending on his realms, from a land he had barely heard of, especially when he discovered that they shared a passion for music. There was a strong streak of superstition in Guntram, too. He had been terrified when his troops had recently looted churches. 'How can we expect to win a victory nowadays', he asked, 'when we no longer keep to the conventions of our forefathers? They used to build churches, for they placed all their hopes in God, doing honour to His martyrs and respecting His priesthood.'[5] During the next few days, while the Irish were guests at court, Guntram came to appreciate that Columbanus was a gift from God and must be respected, his learning and skills used for the benefit of the kingdom. He must be given an offer he couldn't refuse.

What it was that Guntram offered Columbanus, Jonas does not say, but it must have been something big. A temporary post at court, perhaps, with a promise to install him as a bishop when a vacancy occurred. Maybe Columbanus could succeed Gregory in the metropolitan bishopric of Tours, with its vast secular and religious responsibilities stretching all the way into Brittany and its associations with Martin which made it a favourite destination for all sorts of political undesirables seeking sanctuary. Another friendly bishop of Tours would make the king's life a great deal easier.

Jonas does imply that Columbanus refused the king's offer, and that Guntram, far from being angry, responded by increasing his bid. What an opportunity for Columbanus, an opening in a country crying out for reform and leadership, a king eager to co-operate and give him all he needed. Here, surely, was the God-given chance to carry out his mission, the end of his quest. Together, he and Guntram could move things along, and he could then act as religious adviser to the young Childebert of Austrasia, now 20 years old and recognized as Guntram's heir. They could really make the kingdom of heaven on earth.

But then there was a little voice in his ear. What if this was all

just temptation? He had taken a vow of chastity; did he really think
he could keep it in a court like this? And what had that old woman
said to him at home long ago in Leinster? 'I have sought out this
place of pilgrimage. With the aid of Christ, never since then have I
engaged in secular matters; after putting my hand to the plough, I
have not turned backward.'[6] He had torn himself away from his
mother, left his beloved lake-cradled Cleenish and beautiful
Bangor, and now he was being sorely tempted by secular power in
France. Or was he in danger of rejecting the great work God had
prepared for him, through false humility or even misplaced pride?
How could he tell?

Guntram himself helped Columbanus to his answer. When he
saw that this extraordinary man was not interested in status and
power for its own sake, he suggested a compromise. Stay in France
where you are needed, but do not feel tied to court.

'If you wish to take the Cross of Christ upon you and follow
Him, seek the quiet of a hermitage. Only be careful, for the
increase of your own reward and for our spiritual good, to remain
in our kingdom and not to go to the neighbouring peoples.' As
the choice was left to him in this manner, he followed the king's
advice and chose for himself a hermitage.[7]

Notes

1 Jonas says the Frankish King who summoned Columbanus was Sigibert, who
ruled Austrasia from 561 to 575. He also says that the king 'ruled with honour
over Austrasia and Burgundy'. These statements do not fit the known facts about
the Frankish royal families. The only king who ruled over both Burgundy and
Austrasia in this period was Guntram, who was from 575 the unofficial regent
of Austrasia for his nephew, Sigibert's son Childebert. Austrasia was in any case
too far away from the Breton borders for rumours of a party of religious
extremists there to be of concern, but from 584 Guntram was also regent of
modern Normandy, the lands into which Columbanus had moved.
Furthermore, the site Columbanus was eventually given by the king was in the
Vosges, in Burgundy, which would not have been in Sigibert's power to grant.

   Nor does the identification of the Frankish king as Sigibert fit well with what
is known of Columbanus' own dates. Even if Columbanus was among the first
intake of monks to Bangor after its foundation in 559, it must have taken at least

ten years for him to rise to being head of the school, and to become established in Comgall's favour. St Gall, whom Columbanus had taught, had been ordained priest and was therefore almost certainly at least 30 years old when they left Bangor together. The date for the departure from Ireland can therefore hardly be before about 580 at the earliest. At the other end of the sojourn in France, Jonas says (43, 38) that Columbanus left the Vosges in 610, 20 years after first going there; this fixes his arrival at 590. This fits well with the conventional date of 589 for his arrival in France, but would leave an unexplained gap of 15 years between the death of Sigibert as his royal patron and the foundation of his first known monastery.

Why Jonas should have made a mistake in naming the king is a mystery, but all the evidence seems to point to him having done so, and Columbanus' royal patron is usually assumed to have been Guntram.

2 Jonas, 12 (Munro, 1895).
3 Sulpicius Severus, *Life of St Martin*, VIII (395 AD) (Hoare, 1954).
4 Sulpicius Severus, *Life of St Martin*, VIII (Hoare, 1954).
5 Gregory of Tours, *The History of the Franks*, VIII.30 (Thorpe, 1974).
6 Jonas, 8 (Munro, 1895).
7 Jonas, 12 (Munro, 1895).

10

In the Vosges

At that time there was a great wilderness called Vosagus, in which there was a castle, which had long been in ruins, and which had been called for ages Anagrates. When the holy man came to that place, he settled there with his followers, in spite of the entire loneliness, the wilderness and the rocks.[1]

One can almost hear the elegant, city-bred Italian Jonas struggling to comprehend the choice, but the foothills of the Vosges was an ideal place for Columbanus to settle. Once a Roman pleasure ground, dotted with spas and healing springs, the area had been virtually abandoned since the Germanic invasions. Always thinly populated, the baths and fortlets were tumbling into ruins as the surrounding forests enveloped them again. Without any sizeable centres of population, and off any major routes, it was yet only a week's walk from Chalon and therefore accessible for royal visits.

Their way took them out of the city over the broad curve of the Saône and along the road towards Besançon, a road whose course is revealed today by place names like Beauchemin. Above Dole, the Doubs valley narrows, and becomes more scenic, but correspondingly less easy for travellers on foot. At Besançon, the hills begin in earnest and here they turned north, into increasingly dense forest. There is plenty of wildlife in these woods today, but Columbanus walked through a landscape alive with aurochs, boar and bears, while his nights were punctuated by the calling of the wolves.

At length they emerged from the forest into a more open landscape and crossed the little River Breuchin into the abandoned Roman spa town of Luxeuil. Prospecting further up the Breuchin valley, they soon discovered a perfect place to settle. By the modern hamlet of Annegray, the river flows through fertile flood meadows, flanked by steep and craggy hills. The soil is rich, the climate pleasant and the hillsides thickly wooded. Guarding a fork in the valley, three hours' walk upstream from Luxeuil, they found the remains of a Roman fortlet, long since ruined but its knoll still rising comfortably above the damp meadows around. Only 50 paces across and perhaps 100 hundred long, it was an ideal site for them, and the abandoned fields on the drier ground behind promised hard work and good harvests to come. The numerous trees that had overgrown the fields gave them ample timber for their little church, and hazel to weave for the walls of their cells. Later on, they could add communal huts as the need arose, and a mill on the river nearby.

Once the land was cleared, they would be able to sow the seed-corn they had brought with them, and cultivate the many edible plants growing wild in this generous valley. They could make a herb garden, too, for treating the inevitable fevers and digestive disorders. But for now, they relied on the wild plants they could gather. Nettles there were in plenty, on the old middens and covering the masonry of the ruined fort, and dandelions, sorrel, primrose leaves, clover, sow thistles and wild carrot and cow parsnip to be gathered from the meadows, although the work was slow. For a few short weeks there were blackberries and wild plums in abundance, and bilberries, haws, rowan-berries, crab apples and of course hazelnuts. And always there was the Breuchin, supplying fresh fish at the hands of the skilful Gall. But as the season drew on, the food became more meagre, and as winter set in they were reduced to eating the last of their hazelnuts and the roots of any edible plants they could find. Even the drinks they had made with fermented fruits earlier in the year were little comfort.

Not surprisingly, one of their number now fell ill, with a fever. What could they do for him? His fever did not respond to the willow bark which was often of help and they began to despair for his life. So they decided on a fast and prayer vigil, the ultimate act of solidarity among starving men. So for three days and nights, they abandoned their pathetic diet, and begged God to come to their assistance. On the third day, they began to think they were hallucinating. For, as one of them recalled years later, 'suddenly they saw a certain man standing before their gate with horses loaded and a supply of bread and condiments.'[2] But the man and his team were no illusion. He was an answer to their prayers. He said he had been led by a sudden impulse to take food to the new Irish community, whom he had heard were suffering hardship. In return, he hoped that they could pray for his wife's recovery from a fever which had plagued her for a year. The woman was miraculously restored to health, and Columbanus' community lived on, strengthened in their faith.

Later in that first winter they again grew desperately short of food, and seem to have grown rather tired of eating nothing but 'the bark of trees and the roots of herbs', although as Jonas wryly comments, 'the compassion of the divine virtue tempered the bitterness of the food'.[3] Again they were saved in a wonderful way. Early one morning, a man named Marculf turned up at the little settlement at Annegray, as much to his amazement as theirs. He said he had been sent from his monastery of Salicis (perhaps the modern town of Saulxures, on the River Moselotte), by his abbot the Breton Caramtoc. The abbot had had a dream in which he was warned to send supplies to help a new and struggling Celtic community in the adjacent forests. So Marculf loaded a wagon and set off with some trepidation over the hills and deep into the woods. By dusk he realized that not only could he not make it to Annegray by nightfall, but he was hopelessly lost, in a landscape where every hill is carved up by crags and cliffs and every level patch of ground seems to conceal a bog or a lake. But Marculf was an intelligent man, as well as a faithful believer. 'He thought that if the command was from God, the power of the Commander would show the way to the horses, if they were left to their own guidance.' So he gave the horses their head and, as he hoped, they found a way down into a safe valley. But 'wonderful Power! The horses, advancing, followed an unknown road and in a direct course proceeded to Annegray to the doors of St Columbanus; Marculf amazed followed the tracks of the horses.'[4]

Columbanus took all this more or less in his stride. He believed in a God who did great things, and he had had proof enough of His providence in the last few years. So he gave thanks for the provision of food in the wilderness, blessed Marculf and sent him on his way home. Marculf, on the other hand, could not get over it. Like the people healed by Jesus, he told everyone what had happened, with the result that people began to flock to Annegray, seeking prayers and healing from all manner of afflictions. The wilderness was quiet no more.

Notes

1 Jonas, 12 (Munro, 1895).
2 Jonas, 13 (Munro, 1895).
3 Jonas, 14 (Munro, 1895).
4 Jonas, 14 (Munro, 1895).

11
The Hermitage

*At one time he was living alone in that hollow rock, separated
from the society of others and, as was his custom, dwelling in
hidden places or more remotely in the wilderness.*[1]

Annegray was not isolated enough for the hermit in Columbanus'
soul. Contact had been made early on with Caramtoc's community
at Salicis, and there may have been others in this supposed wilderness, of which all trace has now vanished. Columbanus longed to
spread his dove's wings and quietly escape to a further refuge. At
home, he would have found an island. Here, he went up into the
hills.

The forested slopes surrounding the Breuchin valley were not a
comfortable place to be alone. He encountered packs of wolves,
bands of brigands and, most dangerous of all, she-bears. He once
found a deep cave, which looked ideal for a hermitage, but the
owner – a bear – returned while he was exploring its inner recesses.
What happened next is not entirely clear, but 'he ordered the beast
to depart and not to return to that place again. The beast merci-
fully went, nor did she dare to return.'[2] Maybe this experience
taught Columbanus that smaller caves and overhanging rocks were
safer shelters if you wanted to pray undisturbed; his cave-hermitage
above Annegray is only just big enough for one.

To reach his place of retreat today, one crosses the Breuchin by
Annegray, goes down the valley to Ste Marie-en-Chanois and turns
right to 'St Columban'. Or, better still, one starts from opposite a
small timber-yard near the Faucogney village sign, and walks up
the hill as Columbanus did and as thousands of pilgrims since
him have done. The path begins overgrown and wet, alongside the
watermeadows, but after crossing the stream it turns bravely uphill

through the woods: a wide track marked on either side by large boulders and heaps of moss-covered stones. After a couple of kilometres the path emerges suddenly into a sheltered cleft of a valley, with a little modern car park and a spruce plantation beyond. There is a tiny chapel, and a huge lime tree under which nestles the cave of St Columbanus. From the back of this cave comes a wonderful noise. A boy called Domoalis, so Jonas relates, was responsible for supplying Columbanus with water while he was on retreat in his cave, and the lad got fed up with hauling it up the hill. 'It tired his knees', he said. So Columbanus told him to make a hole in the back of the cave. While Domoalis was chiselling away, the saint got down on his knees and prayed to give him strength, and 'soon a fountain of water began to flow regularly and it remains to this day.'[3] And so it does. The place where the spring emerges from the rock is hidden in a cleft, but the rushing noise it makes is pure music, and at the back of the cave is a small pool fed by the fresh water. Even better, the water has been channelled a few paces down the hill, so it pours into a rough stone trough, cool and refreshing after the stiff climb up the hill.

Columbanus spent a great deal of time at his cave. He went there alone, to perform special fasts. He retreated from the growing community at Annegray, with Domoalis to act as messenger. As the years went by, he also took individual monks with him when they needed particular advice. One, called Antierin, wanted to visit Ireland, so Columbanus went with him up into the hills, together with a young man called Somarius, who told the story to Jonas years later. All Columbanus would take with them was one loaf, so imagine their joy when after 12 days he gave them permission to go fishing. But unknown to them, Columbanus was about to sorely test their faith in his wisdom. For having gone cheerfully down to the banks of the Moselle, they found to their delight some fish, caught and rejected by fishermen. Two were dead, but 'taking three, which were alive, they carried them back to the father. But he said, "Why did you not bring five?"' Afraid perhaps of food poisoning, they explained that the other two fish were already dead, but Columbanus would have none of it and sent them back to retrieve the dead fish as well. Chagrined, they were 'struck with wonder at the fullness of the divine grace, traversed again their dangerous path and chid themselves for leaving the manna which they had found. Afterwards they were ordered to cook the food.' Jonas does not relate whether Antierin was eventually allowed to make his pilgrimage to Ireland, but he implies that Columbanus thought it was better to 'remain in the assembly of the brethren'.[4]

Fish were an important part of the diet at Annegray. On another occasion, Columbanus spent several weeks on retreat with Gall, his pupil from faraway Bangor. After 50 days, Jonas says, Gall was sent down to the Breuchin to catch some fish, but for some reason he decided to go to the River Ognon instead. Perhaps the idea of spending a little time on that river was more attractive than the familiar muddy banks of the Breuchin. Imagine his delight when no sooner had he flung his net into the water than he saw a great number of fish approaching. But his delight turned to dismay, for 'they were not caught in the net, and went off again as if they had struck a wall.'[5] After struggling fruitlessly all day, Gall went back shamefaced and told Columbanus that he had not caught anything. Chastising him for his disobedience, Columbanus sent him straight down to the Breuchin, where, predictably, he landed a huge catch straight away.

Other tales were soon in circulation about Columbanus' power over animals. Once, when the community were running out of leather and were in need of new shoes, he came upon a dead stag in the woods, with a bear sniffing round it. Ordering the beast away, Columbanus went back and told the brothers to go and strip the hide off. When they found the kill, they watched amazed as flocks of carrion birds came up to it and then turned and flew away again without touching it. Maybe there was something wrong with the meat which the animals could detect – killed by wolves, readily abandoned by a bear and now rejected by carrion birds. Whatever the reason, this incident was marked to Columbanus' credit as a miracle by all those who saw it, and was re-told for years afterwards.

He also showed a genuine affinity for animals, the sort of under-standing showed by the Northumbrian Cuthbert towards his eider ducks and otters. To the little creatures of the woods he showed a softer side of his nature, a love of creation shared by so many of the Irish saints but which seemed odd to the Franks among whom he now lived. In one of the sermons attributed to him, Columbanus highlights the importance of a person's attitude to the natural world: 'If you wish to know the Creator, understand the creation; but if you do not understand that, be silent about the Creator, but believe in the Creator. For silent devotion is better and knows more than an irreverent flow of words.'[6]

One of the royal chaplains, called Chamnoald, became friendly with Columbanus, and used to accompany him on his walks in the hills. His fondest memories were of a gentle man,

> wandering about in the wilderness fasting and praying, and calling the wild beasts and birds. These came immediately at his command and he stroked them with his hand. The beasts and birds joyfully played, frisking about him, just as cats frisk about their mistresses. Chamnoald said he had often seen him call the little animal, which men commonly name a Squiruis, from the tops of high trees and take it in his hand and put it on his neck and let it go into and come out from his bosom.[7]

Notes

1 Jonas, 16 (Munro, 1895).
2 Jonas, 15 (Munro, 1895).
3 Jonas, 16 (Munro, 1895).
4 Jonas, 18 (Munro, 1895).
5 Jonas, 19 (Munro, 1895).
6 Columbanus Sermon I.5 (see full text in Appendix).
7 Jonas, 30 (Munro, 1895).

12
Life at Luxeuil

As the number of monks increased greatly, he sought in the same wilderness a better location for a convent. He found a place formerly strongly fortified, which was situated about eight miles from the first abode, and which had formerly been called Luxovium . . . Here then the excellent man began to build a monastery.[1]

Not everyone who came to Annegray just came for help. Many wanted to become monks in the Celtic way, and some succeeded. The *Lives* of Columbanus and Gall are well seasoned with Germanic names, as more and more local people joined the original group from Ireland. Unfortunately the idyllic little hill at Annegray could not hold them all; a second foundation was necessary.

The partly abandoned spa town of Luxeuil, downstream where the valley widens out, was ideal. Obtaining permission from King Childebert, who had by now succeeded his uncle Guntram as king of the Austrasian and Burgundian Franks, they built a church there and dedicated it to St Peter. Leaving a small community at Annegray, who supported them with food supplies, prayers and labour, the new settlement at Luxeuil soon took shape. It was always going to be larger than Annegray, and being more accessible it soon attracted even more attention. The trickle of visitors became a steady stream, and many who came made lavish gifts. Some stayed on, and before long this new monastery, too, was too small. Rather than expand it further, Columbanus opted for a third separate site, retaining control over all three but appointing deputies to manage the day-to-day business. Six kilometres north-west of Luxeuil he found a suitable place, on a low hill overlooking the valley of the River Lanterne, of which the Breuchin is a tributary. There was a reliable

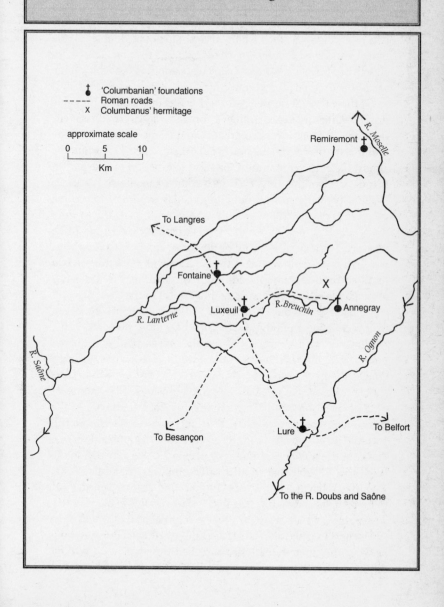

The Southern Vosges

'Columbanian' foundations
Roman roads
X   Columbanus' hermitage

approximate scale

0   5   10

Km

R. Moselle

Remiremont

To Langres

Fontaine

Luxeuil

R.Breuchin

X

Annegray

R. Lanterne

R. Ogmon

R. Saône

To Besançon

Lure

To Belfort

To the R. Doubs and Saône

water supply, and the hill stood safely above the level of the surrounding marshes which in time could be drained and cultivated. To
this place, the modern village of Fontaine les Luxeuil, he sent the
élite of his disciples, 'men whose piety could not be doubted'. Little
remains today to suggest what Fontaine was like, but the priory
church of St Pancras (often a Celtic dedication) is probably on the
site of the original foundation.

Of these three settlements, Annegray was the smallest, probably
not exceeding two dozen brothers. Fontaine was larger. Jonas mentions that on one occasion when Columbanus visited them he
found sixty of the monks out hoeing their fields. This would be
almost the entire community, for all were expected to take part in
manual work of this kind. Even such scholarly men as St Walaricus
(Valery) regularly spent several hours a day weeding and picking
caterpillars off the crops.[2]

Although Annegray pre-dated it, Luxeuil came in time to be
regarded as the mother house of the three, and here Columbanus
was based. Luxeuil was also the largest, with upwards of two
hundred brothers, and in addition it was here that Columbanus
founded his school. At first a training centre for novices, many of
whom later joined one of the main houses, the school soon began
to attract younger pupils, who began with a more elementary curriculum of literacy (using the psalter and gospels as primers),
numeracy, grammar, music, scriptural studies, classics and theology.
One of the first aristocratic visitors to seek out Columbanus was
Duke Waldalen, the ruler of the Jura, and when in the course of
time his first son was born, Columbanus stood godfather to the
infant, who was sent to Luxeuil to be educated. Such powerful
patrons spread the fame of the Luxeuil school far and wide across
France and it was soon acknowledged as one of the very best in the
land. It is probable that another early pupil was a lad called Felix,
who in 627, having completed his studies and been ordained, went
to East Anglia and became the first Bishop of Dunwich.[3]

Keeping a watchful eye on all these monks, most of whom were
newcomers to Irish ways, supervising the growing school, travelling
between the three monasteries and their outlying lands, settling
disputes and receiving visitors, gave Columbanus less and less time

to devote himself to prayer and quiet. So he did what many Irish abbots had done before him. He wrote down some key points for the guidance of his communities, together with guidelines for the heads of each house on how to deal with those who inadvertently or deliberately infringed the 'rule'. It was far from a complete guide to how he believed a monastery should be run, in the way that St Benedict's Rule came to be, nor was it intended for this. It mentions the office of gatekeeper, for example, without specifying how he should be chosen, how important a position it was or even what the job entailed. But Columbanus' Rule allowed the houses, governed by people who knew him, to function for prolonged periods while he was away and it is unique as the fullest and earliest of such documents to survive. Thus it gives the modern reader a telescopic view back over the centuries into the daily life of Columbanus' monks. For almost three hundred years, before the Benedictine Rule became established as the norm, the Columbanian Rule set the standards and principles for religious houses all over north-western Europe and had a profound influence on the life of the wider church.

> *Of Obedience.* At the first word of a senior, everyone on hearing must rise to obey, because their obedience is offered to God ...
> *Of Food and Drink.* Let the monks' food be plain and taken at evening, avoiding excess, and their drink avoiding intoxication, so as to sustain and not harm ... For if fasting exceeds due measure, it will be a vice not a virtue; for virtue supports and retains many good things.
> *Of Poverty.* Monks, to whom for Christ's sake 'the world is crucified and themselves to the world', must guard against greed, for indeed it is reprehensible for them not only to possess more things than they need, but even to want them. It is not what they possess that matters, but rather how their wills are affected by their possessions ...
> *Of Mortification.* The most important part of the monks' rule is mortification; indeed they are instructed in scripture, 'Do nothing without counsel.' ... But though this discipline may seem harsh to the unyielding, that a man should always hang on the

words of another, yet to those bent on fearing God it will be found pleasant and secure . . . because nothing is more pleasant than security of conscience.

Of the Perfection of the Monk. Let a monk live in a monastery under the discipline of one father and in fellowship with many, so that from one he may learn humility and from another patience. For one may teach him silence, the other meekness. Let him not do what he wants, let him eat what he is ordered, have as much as he has received, discharge his own allotted share of work, and be subject to someone he does not like. Let him come to bed exhausted and sleep while he walks, and let him be forced to rise when he has not yet finished his sleep. When he suffers wrong let him keep silent, let him fear the superior of the monastery as a lord, love him as a father and believe that whatever he commands is for his welfare, and let him not pass judgement on the decision of an elder; it is his duty to obey and to fulfil what has been commanded, as Moses says, 'Hear, O Israel' and so on. Here ends the Rule.

Only on the subject of the daily offices does Columbanus go into practical details since, as he says, he knows there are many different ways of doing this. Even here, his Rule merely discusses some of the points of contention over how many psalms to sing and when. He does not actually give a complete order of service, or even a full list of what should be covered each day.

The so-called 'Communal Rule of the Brethren' is more like a Rule in the modern sense. It is a list, with some explanatory notes, of how severely some of the most common breaches of discipline were to be punished. The prescriptions themselves were not unduly harsh, in view of the rigour of the daily regime the monks had voluntarily undertaken, and they were regarded as curative medicine rather than vindictive punishment. Minor offences were dealt with by being struck on the palm with a leather strap (six blows for starting a meal before grace or coughing during a service, 12 for failing to seek a blessing before or after leaving the enclosure, 50 for arguing), more serious ones with fasts or extra work (for paying a visit to the kitchens after hours, one fast; for slandering a fellow monk, three fasts). Throughout, the Rule was leavened by Columbanus' care for the monks he was responsible for, and his innate good leadership: even the normal punishment for laughter in church was to be waived if there was a good reason for the offence.

When set down baldly in black and white, this does not necessarily seem an attractive way of life. But to the Franks it was heroic Christianity; it related directly to what they heard from the Bible, in a way that the existing continental church, so often urbane, established and rich, did not. Above all it worked. In an age when seeing was believing, those for whom Columbanus prayed recovered, and his influence spread. Wealthy Burgundians placed their lands and their sons in his care, and his monks began fanning out across France, founding daughter houses and being appointed abbots of existing monasteries to which they introduced the new Columbanian ideals. Duke Waldalen of the Jura and his wife Flavia remained faithful to Columbanus. Their eldest son, Donatus, became bishop of Besançon and founded a Columbanian monastery. His younger brother was also educated at Luxeuil, and when he had succeeded his father as duke he, too, founded a monastery, while the widowed Flavia retired to Besançon and founded a nunnery there. With numerous examples like these, the flames of a revival began to light the spirit of France.

Notes

1 Jonas, 17 (Munro, 1895).
2 *Life of St Walaricus, Abbot of Leuconaus*, VI (11th century) (Latin text ed. Krush).
3 Bede's *Ecclesiastical History of the English People*, II.15 (McClure and Collins, 1994, 1999).

13

Conflict with the Local Bishops

But as to those bishops who are ordained uncanonically, that is for payment, what, I ask, is your decision? The teacher Gildas described them as simoniacs and plagues. Must we be in communion with them? Because, what is more serious, many in this province are known to be such.[1]

Despite the great interest in Columbanus, the general moral tone of society was not high. Gregory of Tours sadly summed up his generation in the Preface to his *History*: 'A great many things keep happening, some of them good, some of them bad. The inhabitants of different countries keep quarrelling fiercely with each other and kings go on losing their temper in the most furious way.' Many of the aristocracy were breaking all of the commandments regularly, and some clergy were not far behind.

Such was Columbanus' appeal, however, that before long he found himself becoming a kind of father confessor to the nation. The early church had evolved a strict and very public system of penance for those believers who confessed to sins, but as the faith spread this soon became unwieldy and impractical. By the time of Leo the Great (pope from 440 to 461), public penance was reserved for fornication, murder and apostasy; for all other sins, private confession to a bishop or priest was deemed sufficient. This system was clearly open to abuse, and to the suspicion of abuse when those who confessed seemed no 'better' for it, but it was another 750 years before the Roman church formalized an alternative system, requiring regular and specific private confession and absolution involving a priest. Meanwhile, the Irish churches had developed a quite different approach, with regular if not daily confession and discussion with a 'soul friend' demanded of all monks and encouraged for the laity as well. These soul friends and the penitential system they represented were deeply respected; their decisions could take precedence over those of an abbot. A well-known saying, attributed to numerous Irish teachers including Columbanus' own Comgall of Bangor, was that 'a man without a soul friend is a body without a head'.

So what should Columbanus do, when the Frankish nobility came to him to confess to murder, adultery, treason, theft, despoiling of churches, or their clergy unburdened their troubled consciences of unfair or unwise appointments, broken vows, drunkenness, or apostasy in the face of civil misrule? The existing continental system was not working for the Franks; they needed personal leadership and a hard but just code of practice to work to. Columbanus wrote to the pope, explaining his problem, and then set to work to modify the existing Celtic penitentials to the Frankish situation. A major source was the work of 'Vinnianus', believed by many to be another name for Finnian of Clonard, who had taught Sinell, Columbanus' own teacher. This penitential is the earliest to survive and divides sins into eight broad categories: greed, fornication, avarice, anger, despondency, sloth, vanity and pride. Out of these materials, Columbanus devised a manual designed to deter, to punish, to reform and not least to provide some recompense for the victims of wrongdoing. Modern law codes could learn from his breadth of vision. Above all, the penitential system aimed to heal both the sinner and those sinned against. Thus gluttony was punished by the imposition of fasts, and whoever had caused bloodshed was responsible for caring for the victim, paying his medical bills and making up his lost earnings, as well as undertaking a 40-day fast. A homicide was to be sent *unarmed* into exile for three years to teach him the value of human life and after his return was to pay off some of his debt to the dead man's family by working for them. The fixed penalties depended also on the status of the offender. If a priest confessed to drunkenness, he fasted for 40 days, but for a layman seven days was considered enough.

The clarity of thought and the bold programme of reform

enshrined in Columbanus' penitentials met with a mixed reaction. Among many of the nobility it was popular, for to them it had seemed wrong that under the previous system a confessed and shriven warrior could never bear arms again. The bishops were less sure. On the one hand, they admired the new concept of penance and grasped eagerly at the handle it gave them on the moral plight of the times. The idea was widely and rapidly adopted and was formally accepted in the eighth canon of the Synod of Chalon-sur-Saône in 650, when the Frankish church declared that penance was 'useful for all men' and that 'the entire episcopate is agreed that after confession a penance should be imposed on the penitents by the priests.' On the other hand, the bishops were acutely aware that Columbanus, though merely an abbot, had set himself up above the authority of the local church. He did not ask permission of the bishop when a new monastery was founded, but went about church planting, as if in a virgin mission field. He dealt directly with the king, or with the pope, and to make matters worse he had brought an Irish bishop with him, so his church within the church was secure.

But Columbanus was not being deliberately provocative. Indeed it probably took him some time to work out why the hostility arose. In Ireland, the abbot ruled supreme, over an area delineated by his monastic 'familia'. The abbot was the leader, the ruler of the monasteries, the decision maker. The bishops were uniquely qualified men of prayer, who presided at eucharists whenever possible and ordained and consecrated other men to holy orders, but they were subordinate to the abbot, lived alongside the other monks, and had no geographically defined dioceses.

Before many years had passed, the undercurrents of discontent with Columbanus became more sharply focused on one of the oldest and seemingly most pointless arguments in Christianity, one which nevertheless plagued the churches for hundreds of years: when to celebrate Easter. The date had always been dependent on the phases of the moon, because it was derived from the Jewish Feast of the Passover. It was to be kept on the first Sunday after the full moon of the spring equinox. By about 200 AD it was generally agreed that Passover and Easter should not coincide, and there began a series of attempts to produce reliable formulae by which the date of Easter could be calculated. For many years an 84-year cycle was used in Rome, and this was the system, with its papal authority, which came to the early Irish converts. But later on, new methods of calculation were adopted, although the various churches did not automatically fall into line. Gregory of Tours noted that in 577 France celebrated Easter on 18 April, while in Spain it was kept on 21 March, and he cheerfully admitted that on his own authority he elected to keep Easter 590 on 2 April, a week after the rest of the country. Not only were the Celtic churches, of which Columbanus still regarded himself a part, still using the old official 84-year cycle, there was also the further complication that their calculations were made from a different starting point; they defined the spring equinox as 25 March instead of the 21st!

When Columbanus arrived in the Vosges, therefore, the local church hierarchy soon realized that he was not conforming to local practice on this most important and most vexed question. As his manner became more assertive, so no doubt did this begin to rankle more and more. Matters began to come to a head in 600 AD, ten years after he had arrived. For in that year Columbanus not only celebrated Easter on 3 April, a week before the rest of Burgundy, but his date coincided with the Jewish Passover, a scandal amounting almost to apostasy in Gallic eyes. Two years later the Irish again celebrated a week early, and in 603 their Easter once more coincided with Passover. The Gallic bishops summoned a council and requested Columbanus to appear before it. He replied by writing to Pope Gregory and to the metropolitan bishop of Burgundy, Bishop Arigius of Lyons. Then he wrote a long letter to the assembled bishops.

Columbanus was remarkably self-aware. Or perhaps he was good at finding plausible excuses. He could not trust himself to attend the synod to defend his Easter practices, he said, lest he lost his temper and said something he would later regret. So he explained his position in writing, and apologised for his absence: 'I did not dare go to you in person in case I should perhaps contend contrary to the apostle's command where he says "do not contend with words"... Therefore far be it from me to press the need to argue with you, so that our enemies, namely Jews, heretics or pagan Gentiles may rejoice in our conflict, yes far be it from me indeed.' He withdrew his original assertion that the 'western' i.e. the Celtic Easter practice was the correct one and therefore should be adopted by the rest of Gaul, asking instead that he should be left 'to keep silence in these woods and live beside the bones of our seventeen brothers who have died . . . I pray, let Gaul contain us both together since the kingdom of heaven will contain us both if we are worthy.' Columbanus is being a little disingenuous here, at the very least, since by 603 it must have been apparent that he was not destined to live his life far from the centre of action in the quiet solitude of the Vosges. But he concluded his letter with a neat paraphrase of St Paul, begging for unity and tolerance: 'for we are all fellow members of the one body, whether Franks, Britons, Irish or whatever race we are.'[2]

Unfortunately, the synod did not come to a clear decision. It condemned the Celtic method of calculating Easter, as it was bound to do, but failed to address the question of what to do about the Columbanian monasteries. This was not good enough for Columbanus. He wanted to stay in the Vosges, but would rather risk expulsion than compromise on his Easter, which was part of his Irish upbringing, a symbol of his whole monastic approach. The lack of a clear answer could at any moment undermine his authority if the question were renewed. So for a second time he appealed to Rome. Pope Gregory had recently died, and his legate to the imperial court of the east, Sabinian, had succeeded him. To this new pope, as yet unknown to him by name, Columbanus wrote therefore, enclosing copies of his previous letters to Gregory and the synod and asking him for a favourable ruling:

> that through your good judgement we may observe the Easter rite in our pilgrimage as we have received it from our forebears. For it is agreed we are in our native land while we do not accept any of your Franks' rules . . . while we could not do justice to the merits of the case seeing that they (our opponents) are ranting rather than deliberating rationally, we may be able with a judgement to live among them in the peace of church unity.[3]

No reply from the pope survives, but either a favourable one came, or Columbanus assumed that no news was good news. Certainly after this he seems to have felt sufficiently secure to continue to observe Easter according to his own calendar. As long as he had friends at court, and support from the nobility, he would be left unmolested.

Notes

1 Columbanus' Letter (I) to Pope Gregory the Great (*c.* 600 AD).
2 Columbanus' Letter (II) to the Burgundian bishops (603 AD).
3 Columbanus' Letter (III) to the newly elected pope (*c.* 604 AD).

14
Conflict at Court

Theuderic came often to him and humbly begged his prayers . . . for he thought that he was fortunate in having St Columbanus in his kingdom . . . But the old serpent came to his grandmother Brunhilda, who was a second Jezebel, and aroused her pride against the holy man, because she saw that Theuderic was obedient to him.[1]

Young King Childebert did not long outlive his uncle Guntram. He died in 595, aged 25, leaving behind him two sons, Theudebert and Theuderic. The kingdom of Neustria in the west having reverted to Guntram's ward Lothar, Childebert's sons were allocated his remaining lands, with Austrasia and the Rhinelands going to Theudebert while Theuderic was given the central territory of Burgundy. Both boys were under the regency of their grandmother Brunhilda, but Theuderic soon became her favourite so she spent most of her time at Chalon and Besançon.

Brunhilda was a formidable lady. She was deeply religious, founding and richly endowing a monastery at Autun. She corresponded with Pope Gregory, who sent her relics, a valuable book and later granted special privileges to her monastery. She was also involved indirectly in the Roman mission to England: her niece Adelberg had married 'the son of a king of Kent',[2] the self-same King Ethelbert to whom Augustine of Canterbury was sent on his journey to convert the Saxons.

But Brunhilda was also a lady of her times, and accustomed to the realities of power. A Spanish Visigothic princess, she had been married to the Frankish King Sigibert of Austrasia, but he was assassinated in 575, on the orders of her hated sister-in-law Queen Fredegund of Neustria. Brunhilda's five-year-old son Childebert had been taken from her by force and set up as a puppet king in his father's place, while she herself had been banished to Rouen and her daughters imprisoned. She obtained some revenge on Fredegund by marrying Prince Merovech, Fredegund's stepson, who had been sent to capture her, and she survived numerous attempts on her life thereafter. She eventually patched up a truce with her brother-in-law Guntram, who took Childebert under his wing and made him his heir. When Childebert died in 595 after only two years of sole rule, Brunhilda, by now hardened to the brutalities of Frankish diplomacy, was in a position of immense power. She was regent over a great arc of land stretching from the lower Rhône to the modern Austro-German border. The only other major character left on the stage of Frankish politics was Fredegund, now widowed, whose son Lothar was still a minor (see the genealogy on page 46).

The young king Theuderic and his grandmother Brunhilda often visited Luxeuil, and for some time all went well. Columbanus was on good terms with them and visited court periodically. But unfortunately, as the king grew up, he began to show signs of the characteristic Merovingian royal promiscuity. By the time he was in his mid-teens, he had fathered a string of children, including four sons, but showed no inclination to take a lawful wife. Columbanus did not hesitate to take him to task, urging him to marry and secure the succession as well as his own soul, and Theuderic was inclined to take his advice. But to Brunhilda this represented a threat. A queen would inevitably mean a reduction in her own influence at court and make her more vulnerable to her many enemies, whom she had good reason to fear.

Perhaps intending to out-manoeuvre Columbanus, she waited until his next visit to the palace where the king's children lived, and then took action. She led out a procession of royal bastards, the oldest of whom was then about seven, to meet the ageing abbot, and asked him to bless them 'for these are the king's sons'. Columbanus was not impressed, and refused: 'Know that these boys will never bear the royal sceptre, for they were begotten in sin,'[3] he proclaimed. Brunhilda was furious, sent the boys back to the nursery and began plotting her revenge.

She began by issuing orders to prevent the monks from travelling beyond the abbey lands and forbidding anyone to give them hospitality. Columbanus responded by going to the young king, who was then living at Époisses near Semur, to demand to know what this virtual house arrest signified. He found Theuderic who, fearful of causing offence, offered him food as was his custom, despite his grandmother's orders. But to his alarm, Columbanus refused to eat the meal and as he pushed it from him, 'the dishes broke into pieces, so that the wine and liquor ran out on the ground and the food was scattered here and there.'[4] The terrified servants told the king what had happened and both he and Brunhilda, much chastened, came to Columbanus the next day to beg his pardon. The ban was lifted and Theuderic promised faithfully to mend his ways.

Emissaries were now sent out with a view to arranging a marriage between Theuderic and a Spanish princess. But things did not work out.

> Theuderic sent . . . to Witteric, King of Spain, to ask for the hand in marriage of his daughter, Ermenberga. When the envoys had given their oath that Theuderic would never depose her, she was surrendered to them, and at Chalon was presented to Theuderic, who received her delightedly. But his grandmother saw to it that Theuderic's marriage was never consummated: the talk of Brunhilda his grandmother and of his sister Theudila poisoned him against his bride. After a year, Ermenberga was deprived of her dowry and sent back to Spain.[5]

If Columbanus had shown himself to be an irresistible force, Brunhilda was an immovable object when once her enmity was awakened. Who was Columbanus to dictate to her when and to whom her grandson should be married? How dare he forbid royalty to enter the rooms he had set aside for the use of his monks? Having once more subjected Theuderic to petticoat government, she discovered there were others besides herself who had mixed feelings about Columbanus. Many of the clergy still felt strongly about his keeping to his outlandish customs of liturgy and dress rather than conforming to local practice, and some of the nobility did not like the amount of land his monasteries were acquiring. How could a man who claimed to scorn all worldly possessions have the best library in the kingdom and own enough land to form a royal estate?

Once she had a groundswell of opinion with her, Brunhilda felt emboldened to act. She persuaded Theuderic to challenge Columbanus to explain himself and to answer afresh the charges of the bishops of the province. The encounter must have been a memorable one, seething below the surface with the all-important issue of the relative importance of royal and religious power.

> The king, emboldened by Brunhilda, went to Luxeuil and accused Columbanus of violating the customs of the country and not allowing all Christians to enter the interior of the monastery. To these accusations Columbanus answered, for he was unterrified and full of courage, that it was not his custom to allow laymen to enter the dwelling of the servant of God, but he had prepared a suitable place where all who came would be received. The king replied: 'If you wish to enjoy any longer the gifts of our grace and favour, everyone in future must be allowed free entrance everywhere.' Columbanus answered: 'If you dare to violate the monastic rule in any particular, I will not accept any gift or aid from you in the future. But if you come here to destroy the monasteries of the servant of God and to undermine their discipline and regulations, I tell you that your kingdom will be destroyed together with all your royal family.' This the king afterwards found to be true. In his audacity, he had already stepped into the refectory; terrified by these words, he withdrew hastily.[6]

A twentieth-century statue of Columbanus at Luxeuil, by Claude Grange, captures this dispute to perfection. It shows him drawn up to his full height, clasping his staff in one hand, his other drawn back as if he is about to launch a thunderbolt. His sleeves are rolled up to reveal brawny arms hardened by years of manual labour and he stares down, eyes flashing in indignation, at the hapless Theuderic who must be cowering somewhere down at his feet. Columbanus would not compromise. He knew that this might be the final break with the king. He knew also that it might mean banishment or death. The statue shows him wearing his outdoor tunic over his daily garments, and it also shows him with his book satchel slung over his shoulder as a symbol that he was ready for the road.

However Columbanus thought Theuderic would react, the young man's awe for the abbot was more than balanced by his fear of Brunhilda, whose prepared speech he now proceeded to deliver, with as much dignity as he could muster:

> You want me to honour you with the crown of martyrdom; do not believe that I am foolish enough to commit such a crime. But I will follow a wiser and more useful plan. Since you depart from the common customs, I will send you back to the home from which you came.[7]

Notes

1 Jonas, 31 (Munro, 1895).
2 Gregory of Tours, *The History of the Franks*, IX.26 (Thorpe, 1974).
3 Jonas, 32 (Munro, 1895).
4 Jonas, 32 (Munro, 1895).
5 *The Chronicles of Fredegar*, IV.30 (seventh century) (Wallace-Hadrill, 1960).
6 Jonas, 33 (Munro, 1895).
7 Jonas, 33 (Munro, 1895).

15
Exiled

. . . a ship is ready for me, in which I am to be taken to my country against my will . . . Pray for me, my children, that I may live to God.[1]

Theuderic chose not to be present when Columbanus was evicted from Luxeuil. He left the job to a nobleman called Baudulf, who escorted the saint and his faithful attendant Domoalis down to Besançon where he was to stay until the king decided what to do with him. It was a rather half-hearted affair, with few restrictions placed on his movements, and no attempt seems to have been made to upset the routine of monastic life. Probably the king hoped that Columbanus would in future show a little more respect for him, and Brunhilda would be satisfied that he had shown his mettle and asserted his authority.

While in Besançon, Columbanus created something of a stir. He heard that the prison was full of men awaiting the death penalty, so he visited them and after hearing their confessions took it upon himself to let them go free. Domoalis later reported that their fetters simply fell into bits, like rotten wood. The newly liberated prisoners were seen making their way to the church, where they were to do penance, and the guard was called. But when, amid the hue and cry, the guards came rushing up to the church door, they found it securely locked in their faces. The verger was even more astonished, for he had the keys and had the greatest difficulty in making them open the locks. The prisoners begged Columbanus to save them, and the guards, wary of harming people so obviously under divine protection, left them alone. The whole episode gave many people in the city pause for thought, and prisoners and Columbanus alike were treated with more respect as a result.

It soon became apparent that Columbanus was not being watched at all closely. One Sunday he climbed up to the top of the hill behind Besançon on the deeply incised meander of the River Doubs. Now a Louis XIV citadel, in Columbanus' day this look-out point contained the ruins of Caesar's Vesontium. From there he could see northwards, in his mind's eye right up to Annegray and his other foundations. He stayed up on the hilltop all morning, dreaming a little of his brothers, and then quietly made his way down the steep road, collected Domoalis and together they went through the city, out through the gate, and onto the long track home.

Brunhilda and Theuderic were united in their fury, and sent a band of soldiers straight out to Luxeuil to arrest Columbanus and drag him back to Besançon. But for some mysterious reason they could not find him, even though he was sitting in the church porch reading while they searched. The monks were highly delighted, not only to have Columbanus safely back with them, but by this further miraculous happening.

> The soldiers came repeatedly and passed near him, so that some struck against him with their feet and touched his garments with their garments, but did not see him because their eyes were blinded. And it was a most beautiful sight. He, exulting, perceived that he was sought and was not found. While he saw them, they did not see him sitting in the midst of them.[2]

Whether a divine cloud hid Columbanus, or whether the soldiers were expecting to find a grand prelate and simply did not recognize the Irish abbot in his ordinary clothes, the effect was the same. Columbanus could not be found. Eventually the captain of the troop, a more religious man than the others, caught sight of him, and rapidly called his men off and returned to court, to report their failure to the king.

The next deputation from Theuderic arrived during a service, and begged Columbanus to accompany them to Besançon, but he refused. Did he hope that wiser counsels would eventually prevail? He could not hope to carry on dodging parties of soldiers and still preserve the necessary tranquillity of the enclosure. The main body of troops returned to the king empty-handed, but left a small force at Luxeuil, rough and simple men who pleaded with him to go with them. They were torn between their fear of Brunhilda and their respect for Columbanus and what he represented. Terrified, they told him they dare not return without him, nor dare they remove him from his monastery by force, lest the wrath of either state or God fall on their heads. Moved by this appeal, but fearing it would be an irrevocable step, Columbanus at last said he would go.

In this way, accompanied by an armed guard as a last unnecessary humiliation thrown in by the triumphant dowager, Columbanus left the Vosges. The final twist of the knife was the order from Theuderic that all the Frankish monks were to remain in their monasteries. He might only take with him the surviving members of his original party, who were to be expelled from the kingdom with him. Only Gall's older brother Deicola, too old and frail for the journey, was left behind. So Brunhilda was able to have her cake and eat it. The troublemaker was banished, but his benefits remained: his school, now under temporary Frankish leadership, continued to function.

The little party made their way back to Besançon and then downriver to Chalon. Twenty years before, in the prime of his life, Columbanus had led his monks up this way, eager for the challenges that lay ahead. How unexpectedly things had now turned out. Nearly 70 years old, leaving so many dear friends behind him without a proper time to say goodbye, it was hard to accept the reality of this failure. Columbanus tried to cheer his companions on the way, but his own heart was heavy and confused, especially when he remembered the kind welcome and strong support once shown them by the late King Guntram.

On they were forced to go, with no chance to plead their cause before the king, who must have feared he could not withstand Columbanus' appeal. The escort took them over the hills to Autun and then north to Avallon, with orders to get them out of Burgundy by the shortest way. There, a mounted officer suddenly lunged at Columbanus with his lance, perhaps under secret instructions from Brunhilda, or perhaps acting on his own initiative. But he missed, and fell from his horse, injuring himself in the process.

Columbanus made a point of nursing the man overnight and then packed him off home. What they discussed during that long night is not recorded, but at the next stop they were allowed to stay in the house of a wealthy church benefactress and to receive some visitors who came to Columbanus to ask for healing.

From Avallon they were taken down the Cure valley to Auxerre, to join the River Yonne that would lead them to the Seine and so to the Channel. Auxerre was on the disputed border between the lands of Theuderic and his cousin King Lothar, and the Burgundians were jubilant because Lothar had recently suffered severe military setbacks. Columbanus irritated them enormously by predicting that within three years Lothar would sweep away Theuderic and rule over them all. 'Why do you tell me such things, my lord?' asked the captain of the guard. But he would only reply, 'You will see what I have announced if you are still alive.'[3]

Perhaps not daring to let Columbanus loose in Lothar's territories, the escort now did a sudden about-turn, and went south again, up the Yonne and over to Nevers. This tedious detour had added at least a week to their journey, and tempers were fraying. When they finally found a boat at Nevers that could take them down the Loire, one of the guards seized an oar and hit an old Irish monk called Lua, to try and hurry him into his place. Columbanus was furious. 'Why, cruel man, do you add to my grief? Is not the guilt of the crime which you have committed sufficient for your destruction? Why do you appear merciless against the merciful? Why do you strike a wearied member of Christ? Why do you vent your wrath on the gentle? Remember that you will be punished by God in this place, where in your rage you have struck a member of Christ.'[4] The rumour soon went round that this prediction had been fulfilled; as the escort party later made their way back to court having disposed of their charges, this same man fell into the river at Nevers and was drowned, to the horror of his companions.

Meanwhile, the boat took them swiftly down between the sandbanks of the shallow river. After three or four days they came to Orleans, where all the doors were shut against them by royal order. The monks were forced to sleep in makeshift tents on the river bank, for they were even excluded from the churches where they might normally have taken refuge. They soon ran out of food, while the soldiers continued to eat their own rations. So Columbanus sent two of the brothers into the town to try and buy supplies. Having failed, they were returning dejectedly to the boat when they were approached by a Syrian woman who led them to her house. 'For I, too, am a stranger', she said. She gave them food willingly, and in gratitude they suggested she brought her blind husband to Columbanus, for his prayers. The man recovered his sight, and this and other acts of kindness emboldened the citizens of Orleans somewhat and they began to supply the monks with what they needed; but secretly, because the whole city was in fear of royal reprisals.

On they went again, down the broadening Loire, through the rolling countryside that had once seemed so beautiful and strange. Now it tugged at their heartstrings as something dear they were leaving behind, as Ireland had done when they had left her as young men all those years before. All they could do now was keep up their daily round of prayers, to the mingled ridicule and respect of the guards and crew. As the days went slowly by, they noticed how the other men in the boat would fall silent during their services, and some muttered the words under their breath.

Three more days brought them close to Tours, where Columbanus assumed they would stop. He wanted to pray again at Martin's tomb. But when he mentioned this to the guards, their captain curtly ordered the oarsmen to keep in midstream and row on. Columbanus begged him to relent, but he refused. Tours was often thronged with pilgrims and Columbanus was revered here too; his ideals, so similar to Martin's, were being imitated at independent foundations up and down the valley. They could not risk a riot.

Suddenly, in this unpredictable and wayward river, the oarsmen found themselves in difficulties. The boat was caught in a cross-current and no matter how hard they tried, they could not keep her on course. The wind swung round, the boat turned, and before anyone could do anything to prevent it, they were jostling among the other boats near the quayside in the busy harbour. The guards had seen too many strange occurrences on this journey to argue further. They allowed the boat to be moored, and let Columbanus go off alone to the church of St Martin, where he spent the night in prayer.

Word soon got around that he was there, and next morning a message came from Bishop Leoparius inviting Columbanus to break his fast with him. So he went unmolested into the city and sat down with the bishop and his other guests. The bishop politely enquired why Columbanus was at Tours; to his consternation he retorted in a loud voice, 'That dog Theuderic has driven me away from the brethren.' One of the guests, a Burgundian nobleman, expressed his surprise at the violence of Columbanus' language. Rounding on him, the old man replied, 'I know that you . . . will be glad to take my message to your lord and friend, if you serve King Theuderic. Announce, therefore, to Theuderic that he and his children will die within three years, and his entire family will be exterminated by the Lord.' Shocked, the man asked why Columbanus said such things, at the bishop's table. 'I dare not conceal what the Lord has ordered me to reveal,' he said.[5]

Returning later that day to the boat, he found his companions sunk in dejection. A thief had come in the night, and stolen not only their food, but the money they had been given which was set aside as a gift for the poor of the city. Still on fire with indignation after his breakfast, Columbanus turned on his heel and marched straight back up the streets to St Martin's. There he demanded to know of God and the saint if it was right that he should be thus openly rewarded for his long vigil at the tomb by being robbed. St Martin, or someone, must have heard his complaint, for the thief began to be assailed by terrible prickings of his conscience and soon confessed his crime, revealing the names of those with whom he had shared the spoil. They all rushed to return the stolen goods and begged forgiveness. This story spread like wildfire through the city and Columbanus was held in greater awe than ever.

Things now seemed to begin to look up for the little company. The further away from Brunhilda they got, the less the guards restricted the monks' movements. They were allowed to stock up the boat from Bishop Leoparius' cellars (he having presumably forgiven his impetuous guest) and they left Tours in an almost joyful mood. Surely God would intervene in some further way, even at this late stage. Something good was going to happen, they felt sure. A couple of days further downstream was Nantes, and on this last stage the river itself was more full of interest. Ocean-going vessels occasionally came up as far as Tours, with their cargoes of minerals, cloth and leather goods, and these provided some variety from the smaller, flat-bottomed boats like their own, laden with salt, shellfish, grain, wine, pottery and all kinds of fruit and vegetables, making shorter journeys along or just across the river. The wildlife on the numerous shoals and sandbanks, too, was a source of variety: birds they had not appreciated for many weary miles, fishing at the water's edge or resting on the sand; pure white egrets, stately purple herons, flashes of blue kingfishers and graceful white terns. Sometimes the river cut through low white cliffs and then there were martins and swallows wheeling and darting over the water, pursued by arrow-fast hawks. As they went steadily on, they sang:

> We have escaped like a bird from the fowler's trap;
> the trap is broken, and we have escaped.
> Our help is in the name of the LORD,
> maker of heaven and earth.
>
> (Psalm 124.7–8)

As they approached Nantes, the river became tidal – hardly noticeable at first, but before long there was enough flood to reverse the flow of the river for a few hours, something they had not thought about in all those years in the Vosges and which brought memories flooding back of earlier homes, on the Breton coast or further away still by the Lough at Bangor.

At Nantes, a disappointment was awaiting them. The bishop seemed actively hostile. But rooms were put at their disposal, the armed guard that had escorted them all this way returned to Burgundy, and their food was supplied freely by rich benefactresses. They remained quietly in Nantes for some time until the bishop, who was keen to see the back of them, gave word that a suitable ship had come in and would in due course take them to Ireland. It was an Irish trader, which had made the voyage to Nantes with a cargo of British wares and was now loading with wine and other commodities for the voyage home.

One can only guess at Columbanus' emotions as he heard this news. His mind in turmoil, he set to work to write a letter to the brothers left behind at Luxeuil who, now he was so far from them and unlikely to see them again, he admitted to himself he loved with all the deep passion of his nature. Casting off his usual reserve, he poured out his concern for their future in a jumble of disconnected paragraphs.

> He alone who gave it knows the greatness of my zeal for your salvation and my longing for the progress of your learning; but because according to the Lord's words 'tribulation and persecution have arisen for the sake of the word', no other admonition is appropriate for you but to beware of being that 'stony ground' which cannot, from the shallowness of its soil, nourish the seeds it has received ... I was broken, I confess, while I wanted to help all, who 'when I spoke to them, opposed me without cause', and I almost became a fool while I trusted everyone.

The one thing that troubled him above all others was that the brothers should preserve their unity.

> Be on your guard in case there is any among you who does not have the same avowed desire, whoever he may be; for those who have not been of one mind among us have done us more harm ... remove them from office at once; yet remove them peacefully and in conformity with the rule ... Let those who have retained my view of things thus serve God, always electing for themselves the wiser and more godly men, as long as they are humble and compassionate. Whoever are rebellious, let them leave our house; whoever are obedient, let these be the ones who become my heirs.

He appointed Attala as the new abbot, but he was not sure it was the right decision. For one thing, he was not necessarily the man for the job and there had been no time to think through the implications before they were torn away from Luxeuil. Furthermore, even at this late stage he was not sure that it was his destiny to return to Ireland. Perhaps the boat would not take them after all, or perhaps he would be able to make his way back somehow. So he wrote to Attala telling him that if he did not feel up to the task, he could try and rejoin Columbanus as an ordinary monk. But he did not give clear instructions for what should be done then.

I have written this because of the uncertain outcome of events. It has been my wish to visit the nations, and for the gospel to be preached by us to them, but Fedolius just bringing news of their coolness has almost taken my mind off that . . . Now, as I write, a messenger has come saying a ship is ready for me in which I am to be taken to my country against my will; but if I escape, there is no guard to stop me; for they seem to want this, so that I should escape. If I am thrown into the sea like Jonah, who is himself also called 'dove' in Hebrew, pray there may be someone in the role of the whale who will hide me safely, bringing me back on a happy course to return your Jonah to the land he longs for.[6]

Notes

1 Columbanus' Letter (IV) to the monks at Luxeuil (610 AD).
2 Jonas, 35 (Munro, 1895).
3 Jonas, 39 (Munro, 1895).
4 Jonas, 40 (Munro, 1895).
5 Jonas, 43 (Munro, 1895).
6 Columbanus' Letter (IV) to the monks at Luxeuil.

PART IV

Under the Shadow of His Wings

16
To the Court of King Lothar

All, filled with amazement, understood that God did not wish Columbanus to return home . . . Nor did he lack defence, because in all things he had the aid of the Creator, and he who keeps Israel under the shadow of his wings never slumbers.[1]

Columbanus went meekly enough down to the harbour, and allowed all his companions and their few possessions to be put on board. Then, with a sudden return of his customary air of authority, he announced that he would not be embarking just yet. He had found a small skiff, and would be rowed out to the mouth of the river, where he would join them.

Below Nantes, the Loire is a broad, rather unattractive tidal estuary, with mudflats and marshes on either side. Both cargo boat and skiff made good speed on the ebbing tide, dodging between the mudbanks that were increasingly laid bare by the receding water. The smell of the sea was soon in everyone's nostrils, with the wind-torn cries of the gulls. Then, says Jonas, a huge wave came roaring up-river, driven by some unseen power or distant storm. It passed under Columbanus' skiff, but lifted the larger ship bodily up and carried her upstream, to deposit her unceremoniously on a large and muddy bank, the water returning into the channel as fast as it had left it. And there she sat for three days, no one daring to disembark into the sucking, evil-smelling mud that surrounded them.

On the third day, the Irish captain concluded that, like some latter-day Jonah, Columbanus might not be conducive to a smooth voyage. No sooner had he reached this decision than the mud released its hold and the ship floated off. The passengers left the ship as Jonah from the whale, and a shaken captain and crew set sail on their journey alone. Columbanus and his companions, meanwhile, trekked back to Nantes to await developments.

At Nantes, they were close to the border with Neustria, which stretched from Brittany to the Paris basin. There the 26-year-old Lothar ruled. He was a young man with a reputation for being a fair and religious monarch, but one of the few attributes he had inherited from his bloodthirsty mother Fredegund was an inveterate hatred of Brunhilda and her family. About this time, Theuderic had been suffering heavy losses in his wars. As well as fighting unsuccessfully against his brother Theudebert for control of Alsace, he had lost a portion of his south-eastern territories to the Swiss tribes. Consequently he had little time to check up on Columbanus. Lothar, by contrast, had turned the tide of his series of military defeats, and was keen to be revenged on Theuderic. So it was not long before news reached Columbanus at Nantes that suggested he would be made welcome at the Neustrian court. He did not want to remain in Theuderic's kingdom, from which he was liable at any moment to be violently expelled and where he could do little useful work. Neustria, by contrast, offered new fields of endeavour in the familiar context of the Frankish lands. So the little group of travellers set off again, unescorted and at their own pace, to meet King Lothar.

At court, Columbanus was impressed with what he saw. The years rolled back as he met the Frankish king, but there was a difference this time, for he came as a respected elder statesman, in his late sixties, and this king had been in his infancy when Columbanus first came to France. Before long, he became spiritual director to the young king, not hesitating to point out areas where court life was in need of improvement, as well as sharing fond memories of King Guntram, Lothar's godfather and guardian. When emissaries arrived from both Theuderic and Theudebert, asking for Lothar's help in their internecine battle for Alsace, Columbanus counselled him to do nothing. He still firmly believed that within three years they would have torn each other apart, and Lothar would have inherited both their kingdoms.

But life at court had never been a long-term option for Columbanus. As he turned over in his mind how he could spend the remaining years of his life, he longed to be back in the familiar setting of a monastery, where worship and community life were the framework in which God was understood. He also began to dream of moving on further, to Italy and perhaps one day to Rome. The direct route south along the Saône-Rhône corridor was blocked by the enmity of Brunhilda, so he began to consider the alternative, up the Rhine and over the Swiss Alps.

When he told Lothar he intended to leave Neustria, the king was most unwilling to let him go. Several of the monks of Luxeuil had made their way to his court, including Attala, who felt unable to take over as abbot. Eustasius, Columbanus' dear friend and a great scholar, was appointed in his place. With the nucleus of trained and experienced men now gathered around him, Lothar had hoped that Columbanus would found a rival for Luxeuil in Neustria. But although he allowed one of his ablest monks, Potentius, to remain behind and found the abbey of Coutances, Columbanus was adamant that he must move on.

Towards the end of summer 610, the little band set off on their travels once more, this time with a friendly royal escort to guide them. After leaving court, they went by gentle stages round the edge of the war zone; to Paris, which had been liberated from Theuderic's occupation five years previously, and thence to Meaux. There Columbanus lodged for a while with a generous and wise courtier named Chagneric, who listened eagerly to all Columbanus had to say about the future ordering of the church. His son Chagnoald was already a monk at Luxeuil and later became bishop of Laon near Reims. His younger son was also destined to become a bishop, of his home town of Meaux. But his daughter, Burgundofara, was still a child. The experience of meeting Columbanus remained with her all her life, especially as he made a point of blessing her and praying with her before he left. When she grew up she founded a double monastery on the family estates at Faremoutiers-en-Brie ('the monasteries of Fara'), modelled closely on Luxeuil; its fame soon spread and both men and women were attracted there from far and wide. Even the daughters of the kings of Kent and East

Anglia went to school there: 'because there were not yet many monasteries founded in England, numbers of people from Britain used to enter the monasteries of the Franks or Gauls to practise the monastic life; they also sent their daughters to be taught in them'.[2]

Columbanus so impressed his host that when at length he moved on, Chagneric dismissed the escort that had been provided by King Lothar, and accompanied him himself.

Their next stop was only a short day's journey away, on the River Marne at Ussey. There they stayed with friends of Chagneric's, the nobleman Authar and his pious wife Aiga. They had two young sons, and again Columbanus blessed the children of the house before he left. Both began their adult lives as courtiers, but soon opted for the church, and both founded monasteries in the Columbanian style, often choosing men who had studied under Columbanus to be the first abbot. The older son, Ado, founded one at Jouarre, close to his family home, while his younger brother Dado (rather confusingly also known as Ouen) founded several communities, including some in Rouen where he was bishop until his death in extreme old age in 684. In this way Columbanus' influence continued to spread, out of all proportion to the time he spent in a given place, such was the strength of the impression he left with the people he met.

From Ussey, they made their way to the city of Châlons-sur-Marne, and then on through the hills and down to the Austrasian capital on the Moselle at Metz. King Theudebert, the victor in the recent battle for Alsace, received Columbanus and his friends with open arms. He scarcely needed the introduction from Chagneric to realize what a plum had fallen into his lap. Refugees from Brunhilda's repression of the monasteries in the Vosges had made their way to his court, and Columbanus' influence and power were almost legendary. Older and wiser than his brother Theuderic, with a good deal more will-power, Theudebert had had enough experience of his grandmother's machinations to judge Columbanus on his own merits and not believe what Brunhilda's supporters said of him.

Theudebert's territories were vast. To the west and south his

The influence of Columbanus: Monasteries under the Columbanian Rule and sees occupied by his disciples

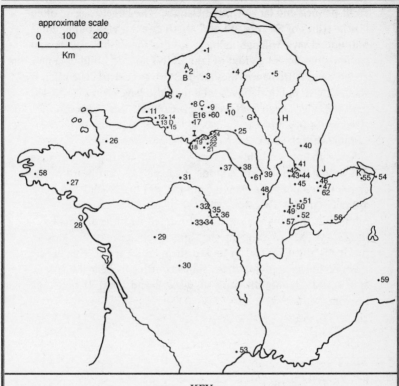

approximate scale

0   100   200
Km

KEY

Sees occupied by Columbanus' disciples	Monasteries under the Columbanian Rule			
A St Omer	1 Ghent	14 Pavilly	30 Solignac	46 St Ursanne
B Therouanne	2 St Omer	15 St Ouen, Rouen	31 Fleury-sur-Loire	47 Pfermund
C Vermandois	3 St Amand	16 Noyon	32 Bourges	48 Bézé
D Rouen	4 Nivelles	17 Soissons	33 Marmande	49 Jussamoutier
E Noyon	5 Malmedy	18 Chelles-sur-Marne	34 Charenton	50 Bregille
F Laon	6 St Valery	19 Lagny	35 Jouy	51 Cusance
G Verdun	7 St Riquier	20 St Maur-des-Fossés	36 Nevers	52 Romainmôtier
H Metz	8 Corbie	21 Faremoutiers	37 Sens	53 Caux
I Meaux	9 St Quentin	22 Rebais	38 Montier-la-Celle	54 Bregenz
J Basle	10 Laon	23 Jouarre	39 Langres	55 St Gallen
K Constance	11 Montèvilliers	24 Reuil en Brie	40 St Dié	56 Disentis
L Besançon	12 St Wandrille	25 Hautvillers	41 Remiremont	57 St Oyend (St Claude)
	13 Jumièges	26 Coutances	42 Fontaine	58 Quimper
		27 Locminé	43 Luxeuil	59 Bobbio
		28 Noirmoutiers	44 Annegray	60 Barisis-au-Bois
		29 Quincy	45 Lure	61 Réomé (Moutier St Jean)
				62 Grandfelden

lands bordered the other Frankish kingdoms, but eastwards Austrasia stretched out on both sides of the Rhine until it came to an ill-defined end far down the Danube. The largely pagan, often hostile tribes of Switzerland and Austria were a vital buffer zone, but not always willingly subject to the Frankish yoke. Would Columbanus accept a grant of land in this area, to build up a new Luxeuil and Christianize these tribes? It was an attractive offer. It was a shrewd political move and it may also have been a calculated personal one. Theudebert well knew Columbanus' reputation for speaking out against the failings of kings. It might be more comfortable with the great man a good distance from court.

Columbanus probably had no clear long-term plan, but here was an opportunity, and he took it eagerly. He had heard of the pagan tribes along the Danube and the idea of preaching to them appealed greatly. This would be a challenge to test his faith to its limits. But the king's suggestion also fitted with the dream of visiting Italy. They could go up the Rhine to the edge of the Alps, to the lands the king had promised them, and then if Theudebert was genuinely keen for these subjects of his to hear the gospel, and would support the mission, all well and good. If not, Italy beckoned.

Notes

1 Jonas, 47 (Munro, 1895).
2 Bede's *Ecclesiastical History of the English People*, III.8 (McClure and Collins, 1994, 1999).

17
Rowing up the Rhine

What the man of God did, as he was ascending the Rhine in his boat, must not be passed over in silence.[1]

King Theudebert gladly gave Columbanus all he needed for his long journey; a team of rowers to supplement the efforts of the monks, a sturdy little flat-bottomed boat, provisions and a safe-conduct as far as Bregenz, at the head of Lake Constance.

Embarking with eager anticipation, the party set off on their pleasantest journey for many months. It was so long now since they had lived an ordered life in a monastic enclosure, that travelling seemed a natural way to live, even if it did weary them inexpressibly at times. They settled into the new routine in the roomy little boat, a group of perhaps 12 monastics and half a dozen royal oarsmen, and rowed down the peaceful Moselle, heading north away from the war-torn border and into the increasingly beautiful landscape ahead. The river was often shallow, the bed sometimes sandy, sometimes rocky, but it was negotiated with ease by the expert oarsmen. At Sierk-les-Bains they passed the ruins of the old Roman fort on the hilltop, then on they went, spending the nights moored to the trees on the river bank or drawn up on a convenient beach. Three days brought them to Trier, where they admired the huge city walls and the massive red and blue piers of the bridge, built long ago by the first Roman emperors of Gaul. Landing, they found their way through the odd mixture of ruins and new buildings to the cathedral.

Trier had been a Christian city since the Emperor Constantine took over this pagan capital of the west and made it briefly into the richest and most influential city in Europe, giving it a bishop and royal palaces. But in spite of its surviving monumental buildings,

Trier's heyday was over, ended with the invasions of the fifth century. The twin pillars of its wealth, the wine industry and the status of an imperial capital, were both long since removed, the vines destroyed by the first waves of invading Vandals and Franks. For a century Trier had been a backwater. Only with the arrival of Bishop Nicetius, who had ruled the city from 525 to 565, did its fortunes begin to revive. He had imported Italian craftsmen to rebuild the churches and the cathedral, he had replanted the all-important vineyards and he had interested the Frankish kings in this once proud city. Half a century later, when Columbanus visited Trier, it was finding its feet again as a trading centre on the water and land routes it controlled.

Leaving the still imposing city behind them, they rowed on downstream for another few days, along the twisting river, past steep slopes newly re-clothed with vines heavy with grapes, until they came into a more open landscape, with lower hills fading away into the distance to the south. Then suddenly the river took a sharp turn, and ahead they could see the most dramatic landmark on the journey, called by the Romans simply 'Confluentes' – 'The Great Confluence' – known today as Koblenz. Before them, the mighty Rhine swept down to the sea; opposite, a huge fortified cliff reared up; to the right was the way they now had to go, fighting the furious current all the way.

Taking it in turns to row, they crept along close to the bank, over the sand spit at the confluence and on upstream, feeling out the back-eddies. Round the first bend, the work became harder, as the hills closed in. It was not only the current that was now hostile; the hills had changed too. Instead of the sun-blessed banks of the Moselle, with terraced fields and little villages nestling by the water, they were entering a land of wild forests, with rocky crags projecting eerily from them. The sudden twists of the river, around headlands fringed with reefs, made ideal launching sites for river pirates based in the inaccessible hills. Whether toiling upriver in the shallows, or careering down in midstream, the Rhine boatmen sang their shanties as much to keep their spirits up as to keep time:

See! Through the waves our cutting keel bites on!
Hewn from the woods along the two-horned Rhine.
Pull! men, our echo answers us; pull on![2]

After the first day of toil, they had only made a short distance
upstream, and the current had become a racing flood, channelled
between the hills on either side. It was tempting to abandon the
boat and walk, along the old tow-path that wound precariously up
the valley. But the king's oarsmen knew that the river was gentler
further up, so they disembarked and hauled the boat behind them,
more glad than usual to stop for each of the daily offices.

The combination of sacred music and the vigorous shanty
running through Columbanus' head led him to muse on the
parallels between this particular journey and his life as a whole. As
they walked, he observed the arduous life of Rhine boatmen, risking
death daily on the rocks and struggling to control their frail-looking
craft in the eddies and tearing currents. This was late summer, the
water low and most of the perils visible. What must it be like in the
storms and floods of winter? By day, kites and ravens wheeled
overhead in the narrow span of sky, by night the incessant song of
the nightingales echoed off the cliffs, in sleep-depriving waves.
Perhaps an alternative to the bawdy secular songs of the boatmen
began to take shape in his head, a song as robust as any sea shanty
but full also of attractive allusions to his own convictions. A
tenth-century manuscript in Leiden contains some verses of just
this kind, which some people think Columbanus may have
composed:

See! through the waves our cutting keel bites on!
Hewn from the woods along the two-horned Rhine.
Pull! men, our echo answers us; pull on!
High roars the wind, the rain storm lashes down.
Pull on, brave hearts and overcome the brine.
Pull! men, our echo answers us; pull on!
Beat back the clouds, the howling wind must cease!
Drive the boat on, our labour ends in peace.
Pull! men, our echo answers us; pull on!
Bear up! Be strong! A following wind will blow.

God guards us still, and He will see us through.
Pull! men, our echo answers us; pull on!
Hated the foe who wearies our poor heart!
Evil temptations, tearing us apart!
Minds fixed on Christ, we shout aloud; pull on!
Keep at your places, laugh the foe to scorn,
Safe from all harm, with heavenly armour worn.
Minds fixed on Christ, we shout aloud; pull on!
Firm is our faith, frail vessels conquer all,
Shipwrecked the foe, his ancient weapons fall.
Minds fixed on Christ, we shout aloud; pull on!
Pull for the prize God offers to the brave,
King, Lord and Wellspring, Ruler of the wave.
Minds fixed on Christ, we shout aloud; pull on![3]

Eventually, singing and encouraging each other, they conquered the gorges. Above the modern town of Bingen, they found the current lacked some of its lower bite, and the river was broader and less hemmed in. Next stop was the city of Mainz, presided over by the notoriously tight-fisted Bishop Lesio. The long haul up the Rhine had exhausted their food, so the king's men went into the city to obtain more supplies. To their dismay, they were unable to get what they required, and returned to the ship to consult. Much to their surprise, Columbanus calmly said that he, too, had a friend in the city, who would be able to help. He went off alone, found a church and prostrated himself in prayer on the floor, as was the Irish custom. Just then, the bishop appeared and enquired who this strange man might be and what he was doing. When Columbanus explained that he was one of a party of pilgrims from Ireland, the bishop told him to go to his house and take whatever they needed. So, leaving only one of the king's men to watch the ship, the whole party went gratefully to Lesio's house and restocked their vessel. The bishop might have been a little surprised at the number of men who made their way to his cellars; for years afterwards he used to tell the story against himself, remarking wryly that he didn't know what had come over him, for 'he had never before given food with so little thought'.[4]

Notes

1 Jonas, 51 (Munro, 1895).
2 From a boat song preserved in an early Berlin manuscript.
3 Carmen Navale, sometimes attributed to Columbanus.
4 Jonas, 52 (Munro, 1895).

18
Detour to Lake Zurich

After traversing many places they came at last, within the territory of Alemmania, to the river Lindimacus.[1]

For 350 kilometres upstream of Mainz, the Rhine flowed sedately along in its broad valley, among hundreds of shingly tree-clad islands. This long section has been changed beyond recognition in the last century, dredged and canalized and its flow artificially increased. But for seventh-century travellers, it offered many opportunities to keep out of the deep water and so, keeping a watchful eye open for shoals and the debris of winter's storms, they could row upstream even with a contrary wind. Columbanus and his brothers could manage this section alone, so the king's oarsmen, who had been so necessary for the passage through the gorges, were free to return to their homes.

For days, little changed in the featureless landscape as they rowed on their way, but then to the left the dark, forest-clad hills began to rise up into the great rolling impenetrable mass of the Black Forest. Not even the Romans had put a main road through there, preferring to ring the massif round with well-guarded frontier roads. At Strasbourg the party probably halted for a while, to visit the church of St Aurelia. They had been promised some relics of the saint, to place in her chapel at Bregenz, and when they made their request they were not disappointed. The custodian of the ancient church presented them with precious relics, which they wrapped in cloth and carried carefully back to the boat in a book satchel.

As they rowed on, they now saw that ahead of them there was something new. Looking like a bank of clouds the first time someone noticed it, rising up higher than any mountains they had seen or imagined, was the awesome, breath-catching rampart of the Alps, the great barrier between Austrasia and Italy. There, in those incredible mountain valleys, lived the wild, half-pagan people to whom they were sent.

At Basle, the river is up under the edge of the mountains. It bends sharply and above this point is too shallow for commercial use; in Roman times the nearby port of Augst (Augusta Raurica) deflected most of the Rhine traffic onto the land and water route to the Rhône via Lake Geneva. Columbanus' instructions, however, were to press on up the Rhine, to a lake at the head of which he would find the old Roman settlement and church which he had been granted for his new community. According to one interpretation of Jonas, that is just what he did. But the *Life of Gall*, which tells the story of this epic journey from a different perspective, adds several adventures along the way, and suggests a rather different route.

Fifty kilometres above Augst, there is another large confluence, and another town called Koblenz. There the Rhine makes another of its sharp turns, just where the broad River Aare flows out of an area of marshy ground to join it. To the occupants of a small boat, none of whom had seen the place before, it would be all too easy to mistake the wider Aare for the major channel, and this, according to the *Life of Gall*, is exactly what they did. Any doubts as to whether they had done the right thing were laid to rest, temporarily at least, when sooner and with fewer problems than they had been led to expect, they emerged 45 kilometres further on onto the waters of a huge lake, curving away into the distance. Awed by the beauty and nearness of the mountains, they rowed quietly up the gentle water, and at its head they found what they thought they were looking for.

Roman Tucconia (the modern town of Tuggen) had been a well-fortified and self-important little city guarding one of the vital roads to Italy, but it had fallen to the invading Alemmanians in the fifth century, and was now mostly in ruins, a shadow of its former self. The Swiss bishoprics had continued in unbroken succession, but the great majority of the population were by now effectively rural pagans, the few remaining inhabitants of Tuggen living on the flat land down by the water's edge. Landing on the beach under their suspicious gaze, Columbanus' little band gave thanks for their safe arrival and immediately set about finding temporary shelter against the chilly night air.

The Irish community had not been in Tuggen many days before they realized the magnitude of the task they faced. In Burgundy their communities had developed a role of leading a nation into a fuller appreciation of the power of Christianity and its relevance to all walks of life. But up here by the Swiss lake what was needed was something much more like primary evangelism. Most people here did not know the most basic facts about Christianity, and certainly had no idea that it might be important or useful. Their Frankish overlords had left them to continue their old religion, and as a result they were 'cruel and irreligious, given to image-worship and sacrifices in honour of idols, and practising augury and divination and many other superstitious customs contrary to the worship of God.'[2]

Columbanus and Gall, in particular, were horrified at what they found. None of their party had any experience to prepare them for living in a non-Christian culture, and they had no precedent for dealing with it. They were determined not to compromise with local customs, so Gall set to work to master the essentials of the local language, and then he began preaching. Choosing to ignore St Paul's advice to start gently, with 'milk', and only to take people on to more solid matter when they were ready for it, he went straight to the point. Aware that his halting speech might fail to carry conviction, he demonstrated clearly what he meant by turning away from idol worship. He gathered up all the carvings and offerings he could lay his hands on and threw them in the lake, setting the temple on fire for good measure.

Gall might have succeeded if he had offered the people a visible alternative to their lost idols, something they could make the focus of their attempts to understand religion in Christian terms. As it was, his dramatic methods only served to infuriate the populace. They banded together and plotted to murder Gall and to expel the other monks from Tuggen. By now, Columbanus may have realized that they had not reached Bregenz after all, and when he discovered about the plot against Gall, his mind was made up. Without delay, they shook the dust of Tuggen off their shoes and, cursing the inhabitants impressively for their hardness of heart, turned inland away from the lake shore and up into the hills.

Notes

1 Walahfrid Strabo, *The Life of Gall*, 4 (ninth century) (Joynt, 1927).
2 Walahfrid Strabo, *The Life of Gall*, 4 (Joynt, 1927).

19

To Bregenz

Thereupon, impelled not by fear of persecution but by desire of spiritual increase, he quitted that stiffnecked and thankless crew, lest in seeking to fertilise their parched and sterile hearts he should waste labour that might be of much profit to well-disposed minds.[1]

Every cloud has a silver lining. If Columbanus had carried on up the Rhine instead of diverting up the Aare and Limmat, he would soon have been faced with the awesome barrier of the Rhine Falls, entailing a steep portage or else the need to continue the journey on foot. As it was, careful enquiries in the vicinity of Tuggen soon revealed the presence of a much larger lake, to the north-east, easily accessible on foot. Was this the lake they had been making for?

The little band set off again, across the passes to the east. They soon picked up a valley running steeply down through a mixture of pastures and forests, and eventually emerged on the shores of a lake so big it seemed like an arm of the sea. They were near a little town called Arbon, once a Roman outpost called Arbor Felix. To their profound delight and joy, a man came forward to greet them at Arbon, with the words from Psalm 118 used by Elizabeth when she welcomed the Virgin Mary to her house: 'Blessed is he that comes in the name of the Lord'. Columbanus, quick thinking as always and with deep gratitude, responded with 'The LORD has gathered us out of the lands', from Psalm 107, which goes on to echo Mary's reply:

> So they cried to the LORD in their trouble,
> and he rescued them from their distress;
> he led them by a straight and easy path

until they came to a city where they might live.
Let them give thanks to the LORD for his love
and for the marvellous things he has done
    for mankind;
he has satisfied the thirsty
and filled the hungry with good things.
                                    (Psalm 107.6–9)

The stranger introduced himself as Willimar, the priest of Arbon.
He and Columbanus seem to have taken an instant liking to one
another. Willimar welcomed them to the little town and lodged
them in his own house while they recovered from the journey. Not
only had they covered 60 kilometres of inhospitable terrain in the
last few days, but the trauma of their sudden departure from
Tuggen was catching up with them. At Arbon they could all relax,
sharing in Willimar's daily round of worship in his church, and
meditating quietly by the peaceful shores of Lake Constance.

The day after their arrival, Willimar asked Columbanus a favour.
Seeing that his guests were far more learned than he, the priest
asked if one of the Irishmen would be willing to give a homily.
Without any hesitation, Columbanus chose Gall, who gave such a
moving and pertinent interpretation of the evening's Scriptures that
Willimar broke down and cried. For years he had been working by
this beautiful lake, almost alone, keeping the faith alive, saying the
daily offices until they flowed like spring water through his mind.
He had made a few converts and was training up a deacon to carry
the torch after he was gone. There had been no spectacular results,
and no dramatic setbacks. Now, out of the hills had come walking
a gift from heaven. Men in wild clothes who spoke like angels. Men
from the other side of the world who were like brothers to him.

For a whole week, Columbanus rested at Arbon. Willimar fed
his guests and took care of their every need. At his request, Gall
preached every day; it was all the payment he could wish for. All
week, in between services and helping out with simple tasks,
Columbanus meditated by the lake. In front of the town, the huge
expanse of water stretched so far that the low hills on the further
shore were barely visible. To the left, he could not see where the lake

ended. But to the right, the mountains piled up, higher and higher until they became indistinguishable from the clouds, their snowy caps sparkling in the midday sun and blushing red at sunset. If he had had any doubts about the wisdom of the decision to quit Lake Zurich, they were laid to rest now. This must be the place to which they were sent.

To make sure, Columbanus casually asked Willimar if he knew any place nearby where they might settle and build a small monastery. Delighted to hear that his new friends might be staying, Willimar replied without any hesitation,

> 'In the wilderness hard by is a place where are yet to be seen ruins of ancient buildings; the soil is rich and well-suited for crops; there are lofty mountains around, and adjoining the town is a wide and level expanse of waste land which will not deny to such as seek a living the fruits of their toil.' After adding much more in praise of the place, he told them it was called Brigantium.[2]

Brigantium! Now Columbanus knew without a shadow of doubt that he was still under God's protection, safe in the shadow of his wings. How else could he have escaped from Tuggen, brought his party up rivers and across unknown mountains, day after day, to emerge onto Lake Constance so close to the place they had been promised, just where Willimar was waiting to welcome them?

Joyfully, they accepted Willimar's offer of a boat, and loaded into it enough supplies for their first weeks. Guided by Willimar's deacon, they rowed along the lake shore, past reedbeds and rocky spits, and past the curious cluster of rivers flowing sluggishly out to the lake. The deacon assured Columbanus that most of these were really one single river, divided only for the last short distance. Where the hills began, the river was united, broad and good for fishing. It was called the Rhine and along its flat valley ran the highway to Italy.

Notes

1 Walahfrid Strabo, *The Life of Gall*, 5 (Joynt, 1927).
2 Walahfrid Strabo, *The Life of Gall*, 5 (Joynt, 1927).

20
Two Years in Bregenz

*Many were converted then, by the preaching of the holy man,
and turning to the learning and faith of Christ, were baptised
by him. Others, who were already baptised but still lived in the
heathenish unbelief, like a good shepherd, he again led by his
words to the faith and into the bosom of the church.*[1]

At Bregenz, Columbanus found the ruins of the city of
Brigantium, nestling close to the lake shore by the foothills of the
high Alps. The site was perfect for a monastery, just as Willimar
had promised. The Irishmen set to work and built huts; on the rich
alluvial soil below their settlement, they planted an orchard and
cultivated a kitchen garden. Gall, who had never forgotten
Columbanus' fishing lessons from the old days in Annegray, made
nets and spent many happy hours out on the lake. He caught so
much fish that he was not only able to keep the community well
supplied, but they could also offer food to the visitors who began
to appear at their gates. Supplied with grain by Willimar until their
own first crops were ready for harvest, this was like Annegray again
but without the periods of desperate want.

There had been a Christian community in Bregenz before, and
the chapel of St Aurelia was still standing. The worship that went
on inside, however, was a curious mixture. On the walls, the people
had fixed large gilt bronze statues and to these they made offerings.
'These are the old gods', they said, 'the former guardians of this
place, and it is by their aid that we and ours have been kept alive
to this day.'[2] Gall and Columbanus had learnt from the hostile
reception they had received in Tuggen. Gall set to work to learn the
local dialect and when he had mastered it adequately, Columbanus

announced that the monks would be joining the local populace for their next major religious festival.

On the appointed day, an unusually large crowd turned out, interested to see what would happen. As the rites were about to begin, Gall stood up and asked for a hearing. He explained why the church was there, and that it had originally been dedicated to St Aurelia, who had worshipped the same Holy Trinity that the monks worshipped. He assured his audience that their idols were impotent and had no power to punish those who destroyed them. Then he took up a large stone and carefully and deliberately smashed the three great idols, and threw the pieces into the lake, where local superstition held a fearsome demon lurked. To the amazement of the crowd, neither Gall nor any of his companions were struck dumb or turned to stone. Some people were angered by what had been done, but many were inclined to listen to the new teachers. Instead of the old idols, Columbanus installed the relics they had brought with them from Strasbourg, with as much ceremony as they could manage. The altar and chapel were solemnly re-dedicated, and in a candle-lit service of processions and chanting, the holy relics were enshrined on the altar to serve as a focus for worship.

Slowly, the little community at Bregenz grew. Progress with the teaching work among the locals was not easy, for these people still believed in their old gods. One day, when Columbanus was walking in the hills, he came upon a group of men about to make an offering to Woden. They had a large beer barrel around which they had gathered. When they told him what they were proposing to do, Jonas says, 'he breathed on the cask'. Probably this was accompanied by a shout of anguish, and perhaps a more direct assault, for the result was that the barrel broke open with an ear-splitting crash, and all the beer ran out over the ground. The onlookers were most impressed at the strength of this old man, that he could burst open their cask so easily. Columbanus, however, was more concerned to direct their attention away from himself, and curtly ordered them to give up these foolish and futile practices.

For two years, the little monastery prospered. The local people did not always understand the monks who had suddenly arrived in their midst, but the local Duke, Gunzo, was under orders from King Theudebert to support the monastery and so it was protected from harm. Bregenz was a beautiful place to live. The site Columbanus had chosen for the monastic enclosure was a little way up the hill, next to the chapel of St Aurelia. It was probably where the modern church of St Gall now stands, beautifully restored but hidden in a maze of narrow one-way streets: Romanstrasse, Gallustrasse, Kolumbanstrasse. From here, there was a panoramic view, out over the lake back to Arbon and round to the left to the mountains which pile up higher and higher to the Säntis massif. And always there was the Rhine, its valley cutting down through the mountains to the lake, the valley that stretched invitingly southwards from so close to Columbanus' gate. Once, he wondered seriously about leaving Bregenz, and going to the Slavs, but he had a dream in which an angel showed him how huge the world was, and how small a part in it he could play. So he took this as an omen, and waited at Bregenz.

Sometime during this period, Columbanus passed his seventieth birthday. By any standards he had had an active life, and he was now quite an old man, although still vigorous. As well as running the little community by Lake Constance, he was back in touch with events at Luxeuil, thanks to occasional visits from Abbot Eustasius. Other visitors arrived, too, bringing news or seeking advice. To several of these visitors he gave letters, to deliver to his various favourite disciples, who were realizing they might not see him again. Among these may have been the letter he wrote to an unknown young friend:

Although I have already spoken for a long time on character and moral training, my son who requires instruction, you ask again to be taught . . . Be ready to serve in humility and most humble in authority; be simple in faith but well-educated in behaviour; rigorous in what concerns you but tolerant in what concerns others; hard in times of ease but easy in times of hardship . . . Though weary yet not giving up; at the same time weeping and rejoicing for zeal and hope; always fearing for the end though moving forward with certainty. See, here is your model, beloved boy and dear servant; if you are like this you will be exceedingly blessed, because you will be the same in good times and in bad.[3]

Notes

1 Jonas, 53 (Munro, 1895).
2 Walahfrid Strabo, *The Life of Gall*, 6 (Joynt, 1927).
3 Columbanus' Letter (VI) to a Young Friend (date unknown).

21
The Death of Brunhilda

In the meantime, a compact of peace which Theuderic and Theudebert had made was broken, and each one, priding himself on the strength of his followers, endeavoured to kill the other.[1]

In the spring of 612, alarming news reached Columbanus at Bregenz. The brothers Theudebert and Theuderic were threatening war again. Columbanus had a terrible premonition of what was going to happen, and felt impelled to act. To the consternation of his community, he took a boat and a couple of companions, and sailed off down Lake Constance to warn Theudebert. They navigated the narrows at the end of the lake, crossed the Untersee and went down the Rhine. They portaged around the terrible Rhine Falls and rowed on their way, in the spring flood waters. Seeking news at Basel, Strasbourg and other cities along the way, they eventually located King Theudebert and went into his presence. Columbanus delivered his message to the surprised king: Theudebert must abdicate at once, and enter a monastery, or he would lose both his throne and his life. The court shook with laughter at the unworldliness of this backwoods monk. Who had ever heard of a Frankish king voluntarily giving up his throne? Or who could imagine a monarch becoming a monk? Columbanus sadly turned and left the young king, telling him that if he did not think again and heed the warning, he would all too soon find himself tonsured against his will.

Columbanus now had to make the return journey to Bregenz, with a heavy heart as he considered the fate that awaited King Theudebert. Hardly had they completed the long voyage back, when Theuderic, urged on by Brunhilda, invaded Austrasia. The two armies clashed first at Toul, near Nancy on the Moselle, and

Theudebert suffered a heavy defeat. He managed to regroup at Zulpich, with allies drawn from other German lands, but there the outcome was decisive.

> It is said that from time immemorial no such battle had ever been fought by the Franks and the other peoples; the carnage on both sides was such that in the fighting line there was no room for the slain to fall down. They stood upright in their ranks, corpse supporting corpse, as if they still lived ... Theuderic again defeated Theudebert and cut down his men from Zulpich to Cologne. The same day he advanced to Cologne and secured Theudebert's whole treasure.[2]

On the day when the battle of Zulpich was raging, Columbanus and the monk Chagnoald were on retreat together up in the hills above Bregenz. It was a pleasant May day, and Columbanus dozed off for a while. But in his dreams he saw the battle taking place, and he awoke in distress at all the bloodshed. Chagnoald begged him to pray for victory for their patron King Theudebert, but Columbanus reproved him. Events must be allowed to take their course; this was only part of the story.

As Columbanus had so sadly predicted, Theudebert was utterly defeated, betrayed by one of his own nobles and handed over to his bloodthirsty relations. Brunhilda his grandmother flung him into a monastery, and then a few days later had him executed together with his children.

Brunhilda and the still pliant Theuderic now ruled over Austrasia and Burgundy, and they moved their capital to Metz. Word soon reached Duke Gunzo near Bregenz that the community of monks there no longer had royal protection, and he began to pay more attention to the occasional complaints made against them for interfering in local customs. He was especially angered that the brothers were not confining themselves to their enclosure and farm lands, but were wandering freely on the hills, where they might be frightening away the game. The duke began to wish to be rid of the monks, and seeing this the people took the law into their own hands. One night, they broke into the enclosure and stole a valuable cow, which they drove into the forest. Two of the brothers went off to find the animal, and they were ambushed and murdered. When they failed to return, a search party went out, who, 'following their footsteps, found them slain. They laid the bodies on their shoulders and carried them back to the cloister. While they were thus overwhelmed with a tide of troubles, the messengers of the duke arrived and ordered them to depart.'[3]

Perhaps the long arm of Brunhilda may be discerned here; or perhaps it was only a locally organized plot to remove the foreigners from Bregenz. Certainly it was a heart-breaking turn of events. For the third time in three years, Columbanus was being forced to leave a monastery he had built with his own hands, a place where work needed doing. The monks were in despair, but for Columbanus there was one ray of comfort: this clear signal that they must move on opened the way at last for him to go to Italy. They would trust themselves once more to the God of pilgrims, and cross the high passes of the Alps to the Lombard kingdom beyond.

They dismantled the settlement at Bregenz, and bade farewell to those people they had come to know and love in their two short years by the lake. Then, at the very last minute, Gall fell ill with a fever. He felt as if he was going to die. Columbanus was strangely unmoved by his friend's plight. He remembered, perhaps, that as they were leaving Luxeuil it was Gall's older brother Deicola who had been unable to face the journey, or perhaps in his love for Gall he felt this talented monk still needed to learn the true meaning of obedience. He accused Gall of exaggerating his illness in order to be allowed to stay in a place he had grown fond of. He would listen to no excuses. Gall, however, felt quite unable to walk, and begged to be left behind. Columbanus, determined to leave without delay, told him that if he stayed, he would never be permitted to celebrate another Mass until the day he, Columbanus, died. It is a measure of the love Gall felt for his abbot that he kept faithfully to this vow, even refusing a bishopric as a result. For Gall was genuinely ill; after the rest of the party had gone, he struggled down to the lakeside, and managed to get into his boat. He rowed himself painfully along to Arbon, where he tearfully told Willimar what had happened and how he came to be left behind. The kind old priest, seeing how ill Gall was, appointed two of his deacons to nurse him back to health.

One of Columbanus' prophecies about the Frankish kingdoms

had now come true. Theudebert, in spite of his mocking laughter, had lost his throne, his family, his liberty and now his life. It was not long before fate overtook his brother's family too. For Theuderic did not live long to enjoy his conquest of Austrasia. He died, probably of dysentry, at Metz in late 613. Brunhilda immediately had his son Sigibert, her great-grandson, crowned in his place. But Sigibert was far too young to command any respect, and in Austrasia Brunhilda was among enemies. King Lothar, who had been biding his time, as Columbanus had recommended, now saw his chance. He attacked Brunhilda's army, with triumphant results. The combined Burgundian-Austrasian army was defeated near Châlons-sur-Marne, and Brunhilda herself was captured, together with two of her great-grandsons. The boys were put to death on the spot, but Lothar condemned Brunhilda to the most grisly fate he could devise. First he had her tried by a court made up of her most implacable enemies, and then she was paraded on the back of a camel. Next, he had her tied to the tail of an unbroken horse, which dashed her to pieces. Finally, she was denied a Christian burial and her remains were burned outside Lothar's camp. Her few remaining followers secretly gathered up her ashes and interred them in her monastery of St Martin at Autun.

So Lothar, son of Fredegund, had his revenge on his mother's greatest enemy, and in doing so fulfilled Columbanus' other predictions. Theuderic's entire family was wiped out and Lothar ruled alone over all the Frankish lands.

This Lothar, who was strong-minded and well-read, was also a God-fearing man, for he was a munificent patron of churches and priests, an almsgiver to the poor, kindly disposed to all and full of piety. On the other hand, his devotion to the chase was excessive and he took too much notice of the views of women young and old, for which his followers censured him.[4]

Notes

1 Jonas, 57 (Munro, 1895).
2 *The Chronicles of Fredegar*, IV, 38 (Wallace-Hadrill, 1960).
3 Walahfrid Strabo, *The Life of Gall*, 8 (Joynt, 1927).
4 *The Chronicles of Fredegar*, IV, 42 (Wallace-Hadrill, 1960).

22
Into Italy

When Columbanus saw that Theudebert had been conquered by Theuderic, as we said above, he left Gaul and Germany and went into Italy.[1]

Driving across Europe today, it seems incredible that Columbanus could have contemplated travelling the distances he did, usually on foot and unarmed except for his wooden staff. But unless one was extremely wealthy, or on public business, there was very little choice if a journey had to be made. Noblemen and their escorts rode, princesses travelled in litters, but for lesser folk, boats along the great waterways were the only alternative to walking. The old Imperial Post had held the Roman Empire together, but even then there was no reliable public post; St Augustine of Hippo once waited three years before he heard that a letter had been safely delivered in Jerusalem. So it is not surprising that when, for instance, Columbanus needed to deliver a message to King Theudebert urgently, he felt that the best way to do so was to make the 800-kilometre journey to court and confront the king himself.

As for attempting to walk across Switzerland at the age of 70, this too was not quite as improbable as it might seem. At Bregenz he had had ample opportunity to observe the traffic using the upper Rhine corridor. It was one of the major ways across the Alps and had been for a thousand years before the Romans conquered Switzerland and built a troop transport route along it. Columbanus had entertained many travellers from the south, and no doubt he had asked them about the details of the journey. He had a feeling he would one day be taking that road himself.

So when the little party set off south once more, away from Bregenz, they knew that although they faced the huge challenge of the Alps, they would be on a well-trodden path, with many settlements and inns along the way.

Even in early summer, the mountains were awesome right from the start. The snow had retreated from all but their upper slopes, and their flanks were deceptively green and soft, but the sheer scale of them was humbling. For the first few days, their path lay up a broad, flat-bottomed valley that dwarfed even the mighty Rhine in its course. To the right, the mountains rose up in ranks until their heads seemed to touch the sky. But to the left, a solid wall of rock reared up higher than the clouds, jutting up above the fleecy whiteness and hemming the travellers in completely. Not for the first time, Columbanus gave thanks for those Roman workers who had toiled to make his road smooth.

The city of Chur was the half-way point in distance but only the beginning of the journey. From now on, the way got steeper, and there was a choice of routes. At Chur they could find lodgings, in a sturdy city with a bishop and churches, and a welcome for travellers and pilgrims. Guarding a junction of three valleys, it had always been an important place for transalpine traffic, and a source of information about the road ahead. Here, too, the traveller could supplement his food supplies and join up with other groups if he did not wish to continue alone.

A week from Chur would see them over the worst of the journey, whichever pass they chose to use. So as soon as they were rested, they were off again, up the valley with its rushing, tumbling river and then up and up into the mountains, keeping to the main road south. Day by day the scenery changed. In places the road skirted terrifying drops; gorges that seemed to plunge down forever into liquid turquoise pools. In others, the rock faces soared up dizzyingly high above them, with incongruous patches of verdant summer pasture perched on the very top. The psalms were their constant companion:

> God is our refuge and our stronghold,
> a timely help in trouble;
> so we are not afraid though the earth shakes
> and the mountains move in the depths of the sea,

when its waters seethe in tumult
and the mountains quake before his majesty.
                                    (Psalm 46.1–3)

One day, just when they thought they must be nearing the top, a broad high valley suddenly opened up in front of them, dotted with settlements and grazing animals. The vivid green grass and countless alpine flowers stood out in stark contrast to the dark forests around, and laid some of their anxieties to rest:

He makes me lie down in green pastures,
he leads me to water where I may rest;
he revives my spirit;
for his name's sake he guides me in the right paths.
                                    (Psalm 23.2–3)

Heartened, they went on, and soon left this fertile valley behind, climbing now up a series of huge steps that seemed to have been cut by a giant in the dawn of time. Stiff rocky ascents alternated with plateaux on which stood occasional dwellings, and the remains of other buildings from long ago, tumbling back into the rock-strewn grass that surrounded them, all set in a tapestry of flowers. Then came a last half-hour of slow and gruelling climbing, the thin air catching at their lungs and cutting cold despite the June sunshine, and suddenly they were at the top. There was no mistaking it once they were there. Around them were snow-capped peaks, but out of the wind they rested and were warm and gave thanks:

Why did you skip like rams, you mountains,
and like lambs, you hills?
Earth, dance at the presence of the Lord,
at the presence of the God of Jacob,
who turned the rock into a pool of water,
the flinty cliff into a welling spring.
                                    (Psalm 114.6–8)

Before their next office, they had time to make a brisk, knee-jolting descent to the shores of two beautiful lakes, lying in the valley below. Then, along to the far end of the lakes and at evening they found themselves looking down the precipitous descent the other side. That could be left until tomorrow, for its plunging slopes and vertiginous twists did not need the added fear of being caught half-way down in the dark. Once clear of this last dramatic barrier, the road followed the steeply wooded valley down to Chiavenna, where it linked up with another pass. As they walked, they rejoiced at the stunning views that opened up ahead and to the left: mountains dusted with the lightest traces of snow, peak upon peak, catching the changing play of the sunlight on their varied slopes. The hearts of the travellers were light now. Whatever lay ahead, they had crossed this great barrier as if they had won a victory. They felt ten years younger, and the beasts of the forest seemed like brothers compared with the fearful majesty of the mountains.

Notes

1 Jonas, 59 (Munro, 1895).

23
At Milan

During his stay in Milan, he resolved to attack the errors of the heretics, that is, the Arian perfidy, which he wanted to cut out and exterminate with the cauterising knife of the Scriptures.[1]

From the lower Alps, the road wound along the shores of Lake Como, to Milan, the capital of Lombardy. There Columbanus was received gladly by King Agilulf and his Queen Theodelinda. Columbanus' fame had gone before him, and the Lombards also knew what it was to face the fury of the Franks. Two invasions during the reign of Brunhilda's son Childebert had been fought off with difficulty and with great loss of life on both sides. With his reputation for fearlessly facing up to Brunhilda and her family, Columbanus found himself once more made welcome at a royal court.

The Lombards were recent arrivals on the European scene; only 60 years earlier they had poured into northern Italy and defeated the Ostrogoths. At first, the loose coalition of warlords had spread anarchy wherever they went, but in 585, at about the time Columbanus had left Ireland, they had chosen a king from among their number, to restore order. He had cemented the Lombard hold on the region by marrying Theodelinda, daughter of the Duke of Bavaria, the arch-enemy of the Franks. When the first Lombard king died, in about 590, Theodelinda had married again, this time choosing Agilulf of Turin, who became a wise ruler, a fearless warrior but a prudent statesman. Though crowned king, Agilulf was known by all to owe his throne to his wife, and Theodelinda was a deeply religious woman. So at this court, Columbanus was more respected and apparently safer than he had been in France.

Queen Theodelinda was a Catholic, part of the mainstream church. She was responsible for many religious foundations, including the cathedral of St John at Monza. But her husband Agilulf, like so many of the early Germanic rulers, was an Arian. This heretical sub-church taught that the Godhead had brought Christ into being (admittedly before time itself began) to be his instrument of activity in the world. This idea may have fitted with contemporary Germanic royal notions about kingship and been easier to grasp than the subtle complexities of full Trinitarian belief. Agilulf did not cling too tightly to his Arianism. He allowed his son and heir to be brought up as a Catholic. But still the king remained an Arian, and many of the Lombards did so too.

Another disagreement was also threatening the calm of the north Italian church when Columbanus arrived in Milan. It had its origins in a very detailed theological debate generations earlier, but had come to a head during the sixth century. The Eastern Roman Emperor Justinian (527–565), a vigorous ruler who aimed to restore the empire to its former glory, had also made himself the champion of religious orthodoxy. He had attempted to ban some writings of three church Fathers, all long since dead: the so-called Three Chapters, which were part of a long-running dispute about the Nature of Christ. Many bishops in the eastern part of the empire had accepted the emperor's ruling, but in what used to be the Western Empire, the ban met with resistance. The pope had led the western church leaders in defiance, denying that the emperor had any right to interfere in church affairs in this way. But threats to his personal liberty had later made the pope change his mind and he had agreed reluctantly to condemn the Three Chapters. By this time there was a full-blown schism threatening. Later popes, notably Gregory the Great (590–604), tried to play down the seriousness of the affair, which was after all of very little immediate relevance, hoping that in time it would be forgotten. But the Italian bishops were incensed at what they saw as the defection and submission of the pope, and they were determined to keep the issue alive. When Columbanus arrived at the Lombard court, therefore, the local bishops wasted no time in telling him their side of the story, stressing the need for something to be done to bring back the papacy from the error into which it had fallen. King Agilulf, too, was keen for the matter to be resolved, and asked Columbanus to see what he could do.

Here, then, was a new challenge. The Irish church had always been firm in its belief that the papacy symbolized Christian unity, that Rome was the mother of the churches. If an individual man failed to live up to his high calling as pope, it was necessary that he be recalled from the error of his ways. The affair of the Three Chapters caught Columbanus' attention at once. As for the matter of the Arians, this was a question of articles of faith where there were clear issues of right and wrong. Had not his beloved St John set out the doctrine of the nature of Christ and his relationship with God the Father clearly, for all time, with the first words he wrote? 'In the beginning was the Word, and the Word was with God, and the Word was God.' On fire again for God, the eagle spread its wings and soared.

In the affair of the Three Chapters, Columbanus displayed all his passion and impetuosity, without taking time to try and obtain a balanced view. He was aware of this weakness in himself, knowing that he tended to take people at face value and to trust them. His experiences with Theuderic should have taught him to judge people a little more by actions and a little less by words, but perhaps he still believed, naively, that churchmen would be different. Urged on by King Agilulf and by the anti-papal party, he set to work and wrote a long letter to Pope Boniface, hailing him as the successor of St Peter but accusing him of error, schism and misjudgement. Ireland had never yet produced a heretic, he said, but had always held to the true faith; this it was which emboldened him to write so strongly. The pope needed to be on his guard, and must take action without delay. The letter ran to many pages, and through a whole gamut of emotions, the assured and assertive eagle alternating with the timorous and humble dove:

To the most illustrious Head of all the churches of the whole of Europe . . . the Wild Dove dares to write to Pope Boniface: the humblest to the highest, the least to the greatest, country bumpkin to cultured citizen, a stammerer to the most eloquent . . .

. . . it is not presumption when there is an established need to build up the church . . .

Others gladly disparage in secret; I in my sadness and sorrow shall censure in public but my topic will be the evils of destructive

division ... saying to those who are our masters, helmsmen of
the spiritual ship and mystical lookouts: Watch out! because the
sea is stormy and made rough by deadly squalls ... Watch out!
because water has already entered the ship of the church and the
ship is in danger ...

And so keep watch for the peace of the church, help your
sheep who are already trembling as if in terror of wolves, and who,
inasmuch as they have been driven round into various folds in
turn, are, with undue terror afraid even of you as well ...
Therefore, so as not to lack apostolic honour, keep the apostolic
faith, establish it with your testimony, confirm it by writing,
defend it with a synod that no one may lawfully resist you.

... let the cause of the division, I beg, be quickly cut off by
you (in a manner of speaking) with St Peter's knife ... For it is
to be lamented and deplored if the catholic faith is not main-
tained in the Apostolic See ... Therefore I beg you for Christ's
sake, retrieve your good name, which is torn to pieces among the
Gentiles, in case it is attributed by your rivals to your treachery
if you keep silent any longer ... For, as I hear, you are charged
with accepting heretics; far be it that any should believe this was,
is or will be true ... Already it is your fault if you have strayed
from true belief 'and have rendered your first faith void'; it is
with just cause that your subordinates oppose you and with just
cause that they are out of communion with you until such time
as the remembrance of the lost be blotted out and committed to
oblivion. For if these allegations are fact rather than fancy, your
spiritual sons are transformed, in a reversal of roles, into the head
and you, surely into the tail; which is a grief even to speak of ...

But be patient with me, as I deal with such thorny topics, if
my words have in any way caused outward offence to godly
ears ... It is the freedom of my country's customs, so to speak,
that has in part made me bold. For it is not a man's rank that
carries weight with us but his manner of life ... Pardon me, I
pray, for being too hurtful and harsh a speaker; I could not
write otherwise on such a matter. For while I wished to satisfy
truth in all things, aware that I must eat unleavened bread with
bitterness, I have served only God ... Therefore, to return to
that point from which I have digressed, I ask you, because many

doubt the purity of your faith, to remove this blemish quickly from the Holy See's good name . . .

And so the King asks and the Queen asks, all ask you that as soon as can be achieved, everything be made one, that as peace comes to the country, peace may soon come to the faith so that everyone one after the other may become one flock of Christ. Let the king follow the King, you follow Peter, and the whole church follow you . . .[2]

After this great outpouring of anguish, a mysterious silence descends on the affair of the Three Chapters, at least as far as Columbanus is concerned. No reply from Pope Boniface survives, which is perhaps just as well. Probably Columbanus became aware of the other side of the story, and realized that the papacy had not, after all, sunk into grave heresy. Instead, the pope was adopting a pragmatic solution to an unpleasant and rather pointless quarrel that was doing no one any good except the opponents of the faith. By stirring things up as he had done, Columbanus had not assisted this process; indeed, as he was himself ready to concede, he had behaved more like a noisy pigeon than a reconciling dove.

Against the Arians, by contrast, Columbanus composed a treatise which Jonas described as 'excellent and learned'. Unfortunately, no copy of it is known to survive. As long as he stayed in Milan, Columbanus continued to teach actively in favour of the mainstream Christian beliefs, and consistently opposed the Arian viewpoint. He did so with dignity, and he never lost the goodwill of King Agilulf, even though to preach against Arianism might be construed as an attack on the king. He was soon in great demand as a preacher, and he warmed to this new opportunity. He must have been aware of the immense privilege of preaching in Milan, a city which since the days of St Ambrose (bishop 374–397) had been one of the chief bishoprics of Christendom. Thirteen short sermons or 'instructions' attributed to Columbanus survive, catalogued in the ninth century in the St Gall library in Switzerland. They are on diverse subjects, from the nature of faith in the Trinity (perhaps aimed specifically at the Arians[3]) to the need for perseverance in temptation, and show him in a range of moods, from the vibrantly charismatic to the quiet mysticism of his solitary hermitages. In one, he compares human life to a journey, and he seems to be drawing extensively on his recent experiences:

> For it is no advantage for you to reach the height you have reached unless you escape what remains. For this life must be thought of as a road and something of an ascent. Let us not ask on the road what will be in our homeland; for toil and weariness are the occupation on our journey while rest and security are prepared in our home country. Therefore we must be on our guard lest we are perhaps careless on the way and do not reach our true home.[4]

The almost wistful strain is seldom far below the surface. In all the excitement and bustle of Milan city life, how much was Columbanus longing for the tranquil regularity of the monastery? How much did he miss his brothers of Luxeuil, especially when a visitor from Burgundy came to Lombardy to see him and bring him news? Was he perhaps becoming aware of the extent of his error of judgement in the letter he had so dramatically dashed off to Pope Boniface? What would gladden his heart now, above all else, was to find a place away from the city, where he could build a little enclosure and retire with his followers; the survivors of the band from Bregenz and the men who had attached themselves to him since his arrival in Milan. He did not want to end his days as a worn-out hanger-on at court. He wanted to find again the peace he had known at Annegray.

King Agilulf, like King Guntram before him, was delighted with the idea. He knew that Columbanus' foundations north of the Alps were becoming centres of learning and stability, producing great bishops, wise statesmen and a more prosperous and just society. Now there could be one of these centres of excellence in the Lombard lands too. He encouraged Columbanus to ask among his friends at court, and select a site for his new foundation.

Notes

1 Jonas, 59 (Munro, 1895).
2 Columbanus' Letter (V) to Pope Boniface (613 AD).
3 See full text in Appendix.
4 Columbanus' Sermon V.

PART V

As a Dove to the Dovecote

24
Bobbio

At that time a man named Jocundus appeared before the king and announced that he knew of a church of the holy apostle Peter, in a lonely spot in the Apennines; the place had many advantages, it was unusually fertile, the water was full of fishes; it had long been called Bobbio, from the brook that flowed by it.[1]

When Columbanus first heard about Bobbio, he longed to go and see it. It sounded to be exactly what he was looking for. And so it proved.

From Milan, he set off to Piacenza with a sizeable party of companions who wished to join him in his new endeavour. Crossing the River Po on the Roman bridge, they took the high road out of Piacenza to the south, and crossed the shoulder of land above the city before dipping down into the Trebbia valley at Rivergaro. At that point, the hills converged on either side and the way became more tortuous, twisting along the rapidly rising valley, until after a two-day journey they came round a corner and the guides pointed to the hillside ahead: Bobbio.

Green woods and fertile green fields around the tiny settlement clinging to the hillside; green hues in the rocks and green foaming water in the river below. It was the perfect place for a man from the emerald isle. Today, this last bend in the road before Bobbio is presided over by a tranquil statue of Columbanus, so different from the ones at Luxeuil and Bregenz, with a dove resting on his shoulder as his upraised hand blesses the approaching traveller. When Columbanus first saw Bobbio, it consisted of a few houses, a ruined church, and some salt works across the valley.

Columbanus sent a message back to King Agilulf: this would

indeed be a suitable place to settle. The royal gift of the land was soon confirmed with a charter, a late copy of which still survives. It granted full rights to all the land within a radius of four Roman miles (about six kilometres), the church of St Peter and half the income from the saline well, which had already been given to a Lombard nobleman named Sundrarit. The only condition King Agilulf attached to his grant was that the monastery was to pray daily for the stability and prosperity of his kingdom.

The church was in ruins, so, as he had already done in Luxeuil and Bregenz, Columbanus began his life in this place by rebuilding the place of worship. Together, the little community restored the stone walls, and cut timber from the hillsides above the settlement for new roof beams. Columbanus led the way in this work, and astonished and emboldened the younger men with his strength and surefootedness carrying the awkward heavy tree trunks on the precipitous slopes. 'Where they had hardly been able to walk before, on account of the steepness of the paths, and had moved as if weighed down with their burdens, they now walked easily and joyfully, bearing their burden.'[2]

The new community were greatly encouraged by the ease with which they had restored the church, and set to work with a will on the other buildings of the monastery. By late 614, all was complete and they could look forward to winter with confidence. The regular routine of monastic life soon took shape, on the same lines as in the Columbanian settlements in France, based on the same Rule and discipline and with the same attention to music, worship and manual labour.

One of the very first visitors to Bobbio was the man above all others who was most dear to Columbanus. Eustasius, now abbot of the Luxeuil group of monasteries, arrived one day accompanied by a large escort of Frankish noblemen. He brought a personal message from King Lothar, and news of life in France now that Brunhilda's family were gone and Lothar ruled in their place. Both Lothar and Eustasius begged Columbanus to abandon his new venture and return to his old home in the Vosges. He had often said it was his most cherished wish to be buried there. It was a very tempting proposition, until Columbanus recalled that if he were to return, Eustasius would have to resign as abbot, a post which he had already shown himself well suited to fill. Moreover, at the age of 72 or 73, Columbanus quailed at the thought of making the long journey back up over the Alps and down the Rhine, even with an escort. And what of the new mission in Lombardy, this last foundation of his which he was just bringing to birth? Students and novices were beginning to arrive here already, just as they had done at Luxeuil. So his mind was soon made up: his place was now in Bobbio, no matter how much his heartstrings pulled as Eustasius talked about Luxeuil and Annegray and Fontaine.

Eustasius stayed at Bobbio for some time, no doubt picking up many pieces of advice on how to run the monasteries. Then Columbanus sent him back to France, with a letter for King Lothar; perhaps he chastised him for his brutal treatment of Brunhilda, behaviour unworthy of the style of kingship he aspired to. Almost certainly he apologised that he would not be returning to France, commended Eustasius to the king and asked him to support the Luxeuil communities. The letter does not survive, but King Lothar took its contents to heart; he 'showed his favour in every way to the cloister, gave it yearly revenues, increased its territory in every direction, where the venerable Eustasius desired, and aided its inmates in every way that he could.'[3]

Even after Lothar's death, Luxeuil continued to enjoy special royal protection, a testimony to the power of Columbanus' name and to Eustasius' faithful labours as his successor. The communities quietly went over to the local Gallic system of fixing the date of Easter, but in every other respect they remained true to Columbanus' ideals, spreading his principles and high standards ever further into Frankish society. Under Lothar's son Dagobert (629–639), the number of monks at the mother house of Luxeuil reached 600. Three major new daughter houses were also founded, taking Columbanian monasticism and its revitalized Christianity still further: at Granfelden, St Ursanne and Pfermund. Dozens of men and women who had studied at these places spread the spirit of Columbanus wherever they went, as bishops, abbots and abbesses.

In Bobbio, meanwhile, Columbanus' health began at last to give way. Lines attributed to him speak of the transitory nature of life:

This world will pass and fade,
Each day we see decline.
Immortal we would be,
But none escapes his time.

From the self-same birth,
And our so-similar lives,
All the human race
By the same fate dies.

Death the unpredictable,
Steals guarded lives away;
Death's sorrow clutches at
Proud doubters on their way.

The greedy who refuse
Freely for Christ to live,
Abruptly lose, while unprepared,
The wealth they failed to give.

. . .

O keep this well in mind,
Whatever beauties pass.
Admire, but do not love,
For see – all flesh is grass!

. . .

In every human form,
The earlier comely grace
Will wane as it grows old,
As sorrows line a face.

. . .

How blessed the family
Which dwells in peace on high;
Where old men do not groan,
Nor piteous infants cry.

. . .

There life is ever green,
Sorrows nor fears destroy;
In joy, when death is crossed,
They see their King of Joy.[4]

As he felt his strength leaving him, Columbanus' thoughts turned
more and more to Gall, whom he had left on the shores of Lake
Constance. The visitors from the north had told him that Gall had
recovered and had moved up the Steinach valley. There, with two
companions, he had founded a small community. But, like
Columbanus before him, his fame had soon spread and he was
now widely revered as a healer and preacher. The settlement had
begun to grow into a monastery, on the site of which the city of
St Gallen would one day rise.

Columbanus now knew that he was dying. One day, he gave
orders that his pastoral staff should be taken to Gall, as a sign that
he had been fully forgiven. The next morning, Sunday 23 November
615, far away in his Swiss valley Gall was unable to sleep after
saying the night office. He called his deacon Magnoald and told
him to prepare for a celebration of Mass. The deacon, astonished,
reminded Gall of his vow not to preside at the altar. But Gall sadly
insisted, saying, 'I learnt in a vision that my lord and father
Columbanus had passed from the miseries of this life to the joys of
Paradise today.' Immediately after the service, Gall told Magnoald
to set off on a journey. 'Set out straight away for Italy and journey
till you come to the monastery of Bobbio.' The deacon was terrified
at the prospect of making the journey, especially in late November.
He 'threw himself at his master's feet, pleading that he did not
know the way; but the saint in reassuring tones bade him not be
afraid, saying, "Go and the Lord will direct your steps."' Somewhat
reassured, Magnoald made his way along the long road to Bobbio,
where he was greeted by the community with the news that
Columbanus had indeed died, in the early hours of that Sunday
morning, just as Gall had believed.

Taking with him Columbanus' pastoral staff, Magnoald returned
to his master Gall, reputedly accomplishing the 450-kilometre
journey in eight days. He also carried with him a letter for Gall,

describing Columbanus' last hours. Attala had been appointed abbot of Bobbio to succeed Columbanus, and it may have been he who wrote the harrowing letter to his old friend Gall. 'Gall, who still cherished a warm affection for his father Columbanus, shed copious tears on reading the letter and told the assembled brethren the reason of his grief; and thenceforward they offered up continual prayers and masses in memory of that sainted father.'[5]

Notes

1 Jonas, 60 (Munro, 1895).
2 Jonas, 60 (Munro, 1895).
3 Jonas, 61 (Munro, 1895).
4 Lines from the Poem on the World's Impermanence ('Mundis iste transibit'), attributed to Columbanus (*c.* 615 AD).
5 Walahfrid Strabo, *The Life of Gall*, 26 (Joynt, 1927).

25
Peace at Last

And so it was that, in the security of his own monastery, the dove came home to rest.

Below Bobbio there is a night-heron colony, nesting on the edge of the river valley. Each morning, the birds fly silently, moth-like, up along the river to roost in the broad light of day. Columbanus, in the light of eternal day, lies in the crypt below the basilica, built on the site of his once famous monastery. Few people have heard of him now, but through his labours in France and Switzerland and Austria and Italy he changed the face of Europe for ever. On his tomb is a serene, life-size carving of him, asleep. And on the side of the tomb, facing the celebrant at the adjacent altar, is the inscription:

Here
In the Peace of Christ, Quietly Lies
St Columbanus
Abbot.

APPENDIX
Sermon I - Faith

A series of 13 sermons or 'Instructions' survive which are often attributed to Columbanus and may be dated to his stay in Milan. No. I, which is translated in full here, sets out the principles of faith.

1 As I bear the responsibility for very necessary teaching, first of all let me say briefly what is the first thing for everyone to know. I desire that what is the basis of everyone's salvation should be the foundation of our talk, and that our teaching should start from that point from which everything that exists arises and from which what does not exist takes its beginning, and that the heart's belief, which has opened the mouths of all orthodox Christian believers to a saving confession, should be the entrance to our talk. Therefore with Christ's help, let our words rightly take their beginning from the origin of human salvation.

2 Let everyone then who wants to be saved believe first in God, the first and the last, the one and three, one in substance and three in character; one in power, three in person; one in nature, three in name; one in Godhead, who is Father, Son and Holy Spirit, one God, wholly invisible, incomprehensible and inexpressible, whose nature it is always to exist because God the Trinity is eternal. You may not seek his origin, he has no end and has always been what he is and will be; because in God there is no repetition, but always the completeness of the Trinity. That God the Trinity is one, God himself witnesses of himself in the law saying, 'Hear, O Israel, The Lord your God is One'. Yet that the one God is Trinity, the Saviour taught in the gospel saying, 'Now as you go, teach all nations, baptising them in the name of the Father and of the Son and of the Holy Spirit.' By this

twofold witness of the two covenants, as on the strongest of supports, the faith of believers is made secure. There you have in truth the unity in Trinity and Trinity in unity. Briefly, then, in view of the greatness of the subject we have said what we believed, and the 'heart's faith' has brought forth 'the mouth's confession'. And this must be firmly held against all heresies, that the one God cannot be divided or separated, because what has been made whole has always been as it is. Therefore let the poisonous and insane madness of all heretics cease since we hear and believe on the testimony of God himself, 'Hear, O Israel, The Lord your God is One', because he who is one has always been exactly what he is; but so that you should know how many, he spoke in the plural at the creation of the world, 'let us make mankind in our image and likeness'. So you should not make a mistake in the number, Christ declares to the Father, the Son and the Holy Spirit, in the name of which God, as of one God, the whole human race must be baptised. What more need be said on the joint existence of the Trinity throughout all time? That God is one teaches us enough. But as to the truth of the persons, Father, Son and Holy Spirit, Christ's division, with the authority of his command, has fully instructed his hearers. By means, I declare, of these testimonies in which the Trinity is proved by being named and the unity by being witnessed, all the perversity of false teaching is ruled out.

3 Since, then, the greatness of the subject prevents us saying more on these matters which are virtually inexpressible, let us maintain with firm faith what has previously been said. Because according to Scripture more will be of no use to the person for whom these few words on God the Trinity are not sufficient. For of him we have said only that he is one in Trinity and three in unity. But who will be able to speak of his essential being? How he is everywhere present and invisible, or how he fills heaven and earth and all creation, according to that saying, 'Do I not fill heaven and earth? says the Lord,' and elsewhere 'The Spirit of God,' according to the prophet, 'has filled the world', and again 'Heaven is my throne, but earth my footstool'? Therefore God

is everywhere, utterly boundless, and, according to his own testimony of himself, everywhere very close; 'I am', he says, 'a God who is nearby, not a God far off.' Therefore we do not seek a God who dwells far from us. We have him within us if we are worthy. For he lives in us like the soul in the body, but only if we are sound members of his, if we are not dead in sins, if we are free from the corruption of a depraved will; then indeed he lives in us, who says 'And I shall dwell in them and walk among them'. Moreover if we are worthy that he should be in us, then in truth we are made alive by him as his living members; 'for in him', as the apostle says, 'we live and move and have our being'. Who, I ask, will search out his loftiest height to approach this unutterable and inconceivable being? Who will examine the deepest depths of God? Who will dare to discuss the eternal source of the universe? Who will boast of knowing the infinite God, who fills all things and surrounds all things, who permeates all things and goes beyond all things, who takes hold of all things and escapes all things? 'Whom none has ever seen' as he is. Therefore let no one presume to seek out the unsearchable things of God, his nature, mode of being and the cause of his existence. These things are unutterable, unsearchable, undiscoverable. Only believe simply yet steadfastly that God is and will be as he has been, because God cannot change.

4 Who then is God? He is Father, Son and Holy Spirit, one God. Inquire no further about God; since those who want to know the great deep must first consider the natural world. For knowledge of the Trinity is rightly compared with the depths of the sea, according to that saying of the Sage: 'And the great deep, who shall find it out?' If anyone then wants to know the deepest ocean of divine knowledge, let him, if he can, first survey that visible sea, and the less he comes to find he understands of those creatures that lie hidden in the sea, the more let him realise he can know less of their Creator's depths; and as is necessary and fitting let him presume to say less about the Creator than the creature, because the person who has not first examined smaller things cannot be capable of dealing with

greater ones, and how should someone who is not trusted in lesser matters be trusted in greater? For why, I ask, does the person who is ignorant of earthly things, investigate heavenly matters? Oh, those who utter empty words, 'not knowing' according to the apostle 'either what they are saying or what they affirm'! For how many – and woe it is to them – who strive to fly aloft on fragile wings and put their own creaturely face into the sky, first presume with impure heart and unclean lips to teach about the great deep without counting the cost beforehand (at least some of them do, not to say all); they do not realise that God the Trinity, who is comprehended by the devout faith of a pure heart and not by the empty words of an unclean mouth is known not by words but by faith. Therefore the great Trinity is to be faithfully believed and not faithlessly debated. For the one God, the Trinity, is an ocean that cannot be crossed or fathomed. High is the heaven, broad the earth, deep the sea and long the ages; but higher, broader, deeper and longer is the knowledge of him who is immeasurably greater than the natural order, who created it from nothing.

5 If you wish to know the Creator, understand the creation. But if you do not understand that, be silent about the Creator, but believe in the Creator. For silent devotion is better and knows more than an irreverent flow of words. For it is somewhat unfitting and irreligious to pass from faith to the empty words of one who discusses the invisible, immeasurable and unseen Lord. For 'the great deep', as it is written, 'who shall find it out?' Because just as the depth of the sea is invisible to human sight, so the divine majesty of the Trinity is similarly found to be unknowable through human senses. And therefore, I say, if anyone wants to know what he ought to believe, let him not think he knows more by speaking than by believing; for understanding of the Godhead will, when it is sought, slip further away than it was. Therefore seek the highest knowledge not by verbal debate but by the perfection of good behaviour, not with the tongue but with a faith that proceeds from simplicity of heart, not which is gathered from the speculation of a clever

unbelief. If then you seek the inexpressible in discussion, 'he will withdraw further from you' than he was; if by faith, 'wisdom will stand in the gates' where she usually lives, and she will at least partially be seen where she dwells. But in truth wisdom is in some measure attained when, in a manner beyond understanding, she is conceived of as invisible; God is certainly to be conceived of as invisible, as he is, though he may in part be seen by the pure heart. Therefore, dearest brothers, let us pray to our invisible God himself who is everywhere present, that either faith's fear of him or 'the love which knows no falling', may make persist in us; and that this fear joined with love may make us wise in all things, and devotion compel us to keep silent on what is too great to speak of, because it is a mysterious and indescribable thing to know God as he is. Who he is, and how great he is, is known to him alone. But because he is our God, though invisible to us, we must nevertheless always insistently entreat him, and often do so; we must always hold on to God the deep, hidden, lofty, almighty God; and we must always beg him through the merits and intercession of his saints, to bestow at least some small spark of his light upon our darkness to shine on our dullness and ignorance in the dark pathway of this world so that he may lead us to himself, by the grace of our Lord Jesus Christ, to whom be glory with the Father and the Holy Spirit throughout all ages. Amen.

References and
Further Reading

Adamson, I., *Bangor, Light of the World*. Fairview Press, Bangor, 1979.

Bradley, I., *Columba. Pilgrim and Penitent*. Wild Goose Publications, Glasgow, 1996.

Chevalier, R., *Roman Roads*, tr. N. H. Field. Batsford, London, 1989.

Connolly, H., *The Irish Penitentials and Their Significance for the Sacrament of Penance Today*. Four Courts Press, Dublin, 1995.

Dubois, M. M., *St Columban – A Pioneer of Western Civilization*, tr. J. O'Carroll. Gill and Sons, Dublin, 1961.

Healy, J. F. (ed. and tr.), *Pliny the Elder. Natural History: A Selection*. Penguin Books, London, 1991 (p. 53).

Hoare, F. R. (ed. and tr.), *The Western Fathers: Being the Lives of SS. Martin of Tours, Ambrose, Augustine of Hippo, Honoratus of Arles and Germanus of Auxerre*. Sheed and Ward, London, 1954.

Hughes, K. and Hamlin, A., *The Modern Traveller to the Early Irish Church*. Four Courts Press, Dublin, 1997 (2nd edition).

Joynt, M. (ed. and tr.), *The Life of St Gall*. SPCK, London, 1927.

Krush, B. (ed.), *The Life of Walaricus, Abbot of Leuconaus*, in *Monumenta Germaniae Historica Scriptores rerum merovingicarum*, iv (pp. 157–75).

Lapidge, M., *Columbanus: Studies on the Latin Writings*. Boydell Press, Suffolk, 1997 (p. 255).

McClure, J. and Collins, R. (eds), Colgrave, B. (tr.), *Bede: The Ecclesiastical History of the English People*. Oxford University Press, 1994, 1999.

Mackey, J. P., *An Introduction to Celtic Christianity*. T. & T. Clark, Edinburgh, 1995.

Metlake, G., *The Life and Writings of St Columban* (1914). Llanerch Facsimiles, Felinfach, 1993.

Munro, D. C. (ed. and tr.), *Life of St Columban by the Monk Jonas.* 1895. Reprinted by Llanerch Publishers, Felinfach, 1993.

O'Fiaich, T., *Columbanus in His Own Words.* Veritas Publications, Dublin, 1990.

Ohler, N., *The Mediaeval Traveller,* tr. C. Hillier. Boydell Press, Suffolk, 1989.

Plummer, C. (ed.), *Vitae Sanctorum Hiberniae II.* Clarendon Press, Oxford, 1910 (p. 7).

Severin, T., *The Brendan Voyage.* Abacus Books, London, 1996 (2nd edition).

Sharpe, R. (ed and tr.), *Adomnán's Life of St Columba.* Penguin Books, London, 1995.

Taylor, T. (ed. and tr.), *The Life of St Samson of Dol.* SPCK, London, 1925.

Thorpe, L. (ed. and tr.), *Gregory of Tours' History of the Franks.* Penguin Books, London, 1974 (pp. 199, 379, 460–1, 509, 513, 557, 558).

Walker, G. S. M. (ed. and tr.), *Sancti Columbani Opera.* The Dublin Institute for Advanced Studies, 1957.

Wallace-Hadrill, J. M. (tr.), *The Chronicles of Fredegar, IV.* Thomas Nelson, London, 1960.

Wallace-Hadrill, J. M., *The Frankish Church.* Clarendon Press, Oxford, 1983.

Warren, F. E., *Liturgy and Ritual of the Celtic Church* (1881), rev. J. Stevenson. Boydell Press, Suffolk, 1987.

Webb, J. F. (tr.), 'The Voyage of St Brendan', in Webb, J. F. and Farmer, D. H. (ed. and tr.), *The Age of Bede.* Penguin Books, London, 1983 (p. 236).

Winterbottom, M. (ed. and tr.), *Gildas: The Ruin of Britain and other works.* Phillimore, Chichester, 1978.

Wood, I., *The Merovingian Kingdoms, 450–751.* Longman, Essex, 1994.